Bert Marsh

WOODTURNER

Bert Marsh

October 1997.

Brent Marsh

WOODTURNER

Guild of Master Craftsman Publications Ltd

First published 1995 by
Guild of Master Craftsman Publications Ltd,
166 High Street, Lewes,
East Sussex BN7 1XU

Reprinted 1997

ISBN 0 946819 51 3

Front cover photo © Tony Boase:
briar vase; 9¾in (248mm) diameter, 7½in (190mm) high.
Back cover photo © Tony Boase:
pink ivory vase; 4½in (114mm) diameter, 4¼in (108mm).

Figs 2.17, 2.18 and 4.27, plus nos. 1, 2, 4, 5, 9-13 and 15-30 in Gallery One,
and all photos in Gallery Two, © Tony Boase.
Figs 1.8, 1.15, 2.1, 4.1-4.25 and 4.28-4.347,
plus nos. 31-40 in Gallery One, by Eric Bignell.
Figs 1.10, 3.7, 4.35 and the photograph on page 46 by Zul Mukhida.
Author photo on p. 1 © Bob Curtis
All other photographs © Bert Marsh

Illustrations by John Yates

Frontispiece by Charles Bastable

Designed by Teresa Dearlove

Typefaces: Avenir and Berkeley

Colour Origination by Viscan Graphics P. L.

Printed in Hong Kong by H & Y Printing Ltd.

Dedication

This book is dedicated to my late mother, Harriet, who had a very hard life. Her cheerfulness through all adversities has been a great inspiration to me throughout mine.

Also to my wife Mary, and my sons John and Peter, of whom I am justly proud.

Acknowledgements

I am greatly indebted to Alan Phillips, who showed immense faith in my work, and encouraged me to write this book. My sincere gratitude to him for making it possible.

Many thanks also to the staff at GMC Publications: firstly, Bernard Cooper, who has not only written the foreword but who, over the years, has reassured me with words of wisdom; Elizabeth Inman who, as editor, has patiently counselled and advised me; and Alex Woolf, who in the latter stages became heavily involved in the editing, for his sheer hard work and dedication. I would like to thank Eric Bignell for his enthusiasm and the pressure he put me under when the book was in its infancy, inspiring me to go forward; and Ian Penberthy, who helped make some sense out of my thoughts and scribbles.

I would especially like to thank my dear wife, Mary, who has been extremely supportive and a very great help to me over the years.

Finally, I would like to thank all my friends and relations for their help and encouragement.

Contents

Foreword

Although five years were to pass before it was born, *Woodturning* magazine was conceived one day in June 1985 when I became aware of woodturning as if for the first time. The occasion was an exhibition of woodturning by Bert Marsh held at the Hove Museum and Art Gallery. I had visited the exhibition in my capacity as editor of *Woodworking Crafts* magazine, little suspecting how significant an experience it would prove to be. From the moment of entering, I was totally absorbed. Never before had I seen, nor have I since, a collection of woodturning by one man in which every single piece, irrespective of its size, nature or shape, demanded attention and respect.

Were I not already familiar with Bert's work, this beautiful book would I think have almost the same effect on me as did the Hove exhibition. 'Less is more' was never more true than in Bert's case. In his hands, wood becomes like a precious material, delicately cut, shaped and finished to reveal its inner beauty. Both visually and to the touch, every piece he creates sings the praises of the material he loves.

I shall always be grateful to Bert for igniting my interest in woodturning and for the considerable help he gave me in getting *Woodturning* magazine off the ground. In the years since, I have come to appreciate him not only as a woodturner but as a friend. Yet I realize now that it was not until I read the manuscript of this book that I really got to know him.

Fortunately for us all, Bert has held nothing back in describing the events that have shaped his life and the beliefs, impressions and techniques that have made him such an outstanding woodturner. What he has failed to do is make mention of the help he has given, freely and silently to so many.

Because he is always his own man, Bert sometimes gives the impression of being abrasive; the impression is untrue. Behind the banter hides a warm and sensitive nature, one that endears him to all who truly know him. At shows, his popularity is plain to see and many are the anecdotes told about his escapades.

What is true is that Bert cares passionately about woodturning and is a formidable debater on the subject, dismissing without fail whatever he considers to be fanciful. Keith Rowley, author of *Woodturning: A Foundation Course*, once told me that the watchword of the old craftsmen was 'Time doesn't matter'. Bert has kept alive this belief. He is tireless in his pursuit of perfection and the ultimate form. In my view and experience, there is no gallery turner anywhere in the world who ranks more highly.

I would like now to share with you a few of the many tributes to Bert's work which stand out in my mind.

There was the occasion when that supreme ceramicist, the late Lucie Rie, was opening the 1985 Chelsea Crafts Fair. As she stopped, with her entourage, to study the work on his stand, Bert said to her, 'You may touch them if you wish'. 'I don't need to,' she replied, 'I have three of them in my home.'

Some years later, again at the Chelsea Crafts Fair, I was present when a buyer from the largest departmental store in Japan told Bert that the work on his stand was the finest exhibition of craftsmanship she had seen in the West, equalled only by the work in one particular exhibition she had attended in Japan.

On another occasion some years ago, Teresa Dearlove, the designer at the time of *Woodturning* magazine, visited an exhibition of Bert's work. When I saw her shortly afterwards, she was full of praise. 'Bert is not only a woodturner', she said, 'he is an artist! His work is lovely, really beautiful.'

When Bert attended a private view of an exhibition by the late and great David Pye, David said to an enthusiastic visitor, 'If you want to meet a proper woodturner, meet Bert Marsh', and promptly introduced him.

My final recollection concerns an appreciation of Bert's work which I believe he prizes above all others. While Bert was exhibiting once again at the Chelsea Crafts Fair, a blind man in his 30s, accompanied by his girlfriend, asked if he could touch Bert's work. Having been given permission, the young man proceeded to pick up nearly everything on display, feeling each piece and asking various questions about them. He even asked 'What happened here?' when detecting the difference of texture where the sapwood changed to heartwood. He finally alighted on the finest piece, a mulberry vase, and asked whether he could buy it. This gave Bert an enormous thrill. He felt, he told me, like giving it to him, but knew this would be inappropriate in the circumstances. 'He went off,' said Bert, 'with his vase in his hand, as thrilled as if he had discovered the crown jewels.'

In writing this foreword, I have been conscious that there are many people who are better qualified for the role. I am certain beyond all doubt, however, that there is no one who could feel more proud than I feel to be given the opportunity to say ... thank you, Bert, for adding to our awareness of beauty and for the friendship which, however many more times we shall cross swords, I shall always value.

Bernard C. Cooper
Founder Editor,
Woodturning magazine

Introduction

As a boy of 14, just beginning an apprenticeship in cabinet-making, I got my first look at a lathe and was immediately impressed by this awesome machine. I was fascinated by the way in which square sections of wood were transformed into beautifully shaped and rounded pieces, by the way the shavings flew, and by the noise it made. I had to wait another couple of years before I had an opportunity to begin turning myself; little did I realize then how developing that particular skill was to affect my later life. At the time my future lay in furniture making, or so I thought, but as the years passed, fate caused my career to take other directions. For a while, I found satisfaction in teaching, but a heart attack put paid to that and eventually led me to pursue a new vocation – woodturning. To me, wood is a beautiful material, and through turning I try to show that beauty to the full.

The four chapters of this book will give you an insight into the important aspects of my life as a professional woodturner: the events that led to my taking that route as a career; my love of wood and my constant striving for perfection; the material itself and how I have tried to understand it; the excitement I get from working it; my own particular way of working and the various stages a blank of wood goes through before it becomes a finished bowl or vase. The photographs throughout the book show how my work has developed, illustrating particular woods or techniques, while the gallery of 20 bowls specifically turned for the book are the culmination of many years' experience and demonstrate the current level of my work.

Achieving success as a woodturner has not been easy, but there is no great secret to my success. It has come about through hard work, a passion for the material, a desire for perfection, years of experience and a natural ability to manipulate both tools and machines, which I was lucky to be born with.

Whatever your reason for reading this book – because you are a turner yourself or because you simply like the look of my work – I hope that it will help you understand the immense pleasure and contentment I gain from turning wood. Hopefully, too, you will be able to share the great beauty of this wonderful material.

① My Life

It took a heart attack and two operations to change my life – from a full-time senior lecturer at Brighton Polytechnic to a professional woodturner. My fascination with wood as a child had led me into a furniture-making career, and then into teaching. When my illness prevented me from continuing, I was fortunate to find that woodturning opened the door to a new life. The road that led to my becoming a professional woodturner has not always been easy to travel; it has required hard work and long hours, and I have had to find the tenacity to overcome setbacks in developing this new and successful career.

In 1981, after many years as a cabinetmaker, then as a teacher of furniture making and woodwork, I began woodturning full time. Woodturning has now become a way of life for me, almost all of my time being spent either turning or in some associated activity: preparing for exhibitions and craft fairs, delivering work to galleries, giving demonstrations, writing articles, judging woodturning competitions, or giving technical advice. Then there is the paperwork to see to – accounts and correspondence – which can be considerable. I also have to acquire the wood I turn, which can involve cutting down the occasional tree. All of this gives me a very busy life and, at times, means working very long hours indeed; being a professional woodturner is very time consuming, and definitely not an easy option.

I was born on 10 September 1932 in Brighton, one of identical twins. Unfortunately, my brother did not survive for long after our birth, and I know that this tragic event has had a deep effect on my life. I have always felt somewhat insecure, as if something is missing, which may explain why I am forever striving to achieve – but never find – full contentment.

My father and his brother were partners in a bicycle sales and repair business, with a shop in Brighton, and later another in nearby Hove. Shortly after I was born, my father, mother, elder sister and myself moved to Hove, where I was to spend my formative years.

When I was about three years old, my mother had another baby boy, but sadly he only lived for a few hours. Then, just before my fifth birthday, in 1937, my father died, leaving my mother with two young children to bring up. She decided that the only way she could keep her young family together

Fig 1.1
The bicycle shop in Hove where I lived and grew up.

was to carry on with the bicycle business, which she did right through World War II. It was a tremendous struggle for her, coping with us and the housework, serving in the shop, and repairing bicycles. Because of the war, new bicycles were virtually impossible to obtain, so most of her income came from repairs.

I have few memories of my father. The most vivid is of him making a wooden greenhouse, which he never finished. I can still see and hear him, planing shavings from one of the parts. These curled away from the plane like magic, which had a profound effect on me, and I am sure that it influenced my choice of career.

I had not been attending school for long before war was declared in 1939. Like so many other children at this time, my education was badly affected by the war. A great number of children had been evacuated from London to the south coast, including Hove of course, and this influx meant that my schooling was reduced to morning or afternoon sessions only, which were held in the local church hall. This arrangement was short-lived, however, when it was realized that Brighton and Hove were also at great risk from bombing, and the evacuees were moved to more rural areas.

I returned to full-time schooling, but this was constantly being interrupted by many visits to the air raid shelters due to the German air attacks. As these raids increased, many of the local children were evacuated from the south coast, hopefully to safer places further north. My mother was worried about this too, so she decided to send my sister and me to live with our grandmother and one of my aunts in the depths of the countryside, close to a small village near Ledbury in Herefordshire. What a dramatic change we experienced: no electricity or running water, and a walk of over five miles to and from school each day.

Fig 1.2
My sister, Margaret, and I when I was three years old.

The small village school had only two classrooms: one for the elder children – the seniors – the other, which was divided down the middle by a primitive movable screen, for the infants and juniors. I was in the junior section. Unfortunately, this was extremely overcrowded due to a large influx of evacuees from Birmingham, who had been sent to live nearby. We were all jammed together and taught by one teacher. Being of various ages and of very mixed abilities, naturally all of our education suffered greatly. Looking back on the shortage of facilities, it seems strange that this school enjoyed the

Fig 1.3
A young boy: this was taken in 1941 during my stay in Herefordshire to escape the bombing of the south coast. Although very homesick, I spent many happy hours in the fields and woods near my grandmother's house.

luxury of two playgrounds – one for the girls and one for the boys.

I found that I enjoyed living in the country greatly; the freedom of the open fields and the nearby woods provided many enjoyable hours, but like my sister I missed my mother and friends back home. Within two years, we returned to Hove and my schooling improved, although there were still regular interruptions caused by air raids, resulting in hours of sitting aimlessly waiting for the 'all clear' siren. There was a shortage of teachers, many having been drafted away to contribute in some way to the war effort. My sister passed her examination for the local grammar school, but when it came to my turn, I entered the scholarship examination with a very negative attitude because I thought that I should leave school and earn some money, to make things easier for my mother. I realize now that this was completely wrong.

A great fascination

When I actually left school in August 1945, I was 13 years old, and I began work on my 14th birthday. From my earliest days – certainly long before I left school – wood had held a great fascination for me. In fact, woodwork had been by far my best subject at school, although I missed the first year of woodwork lessons because of illness. However, due to my natural aptitude for this subject, it was not long before I caught up with the rest of the class and was receiving top marks for my work. So when I left school, it came as no great surprise to anyone that I looked for a job making furniture.

I had considered all the options that were available to me: to become a carpenter, a joiner or possibly a coachbuilder, but none of these held the same attraction as cabinetmaking – I was determined to make furniture. Because of the war there was a shortage of wood and very little furniture was being made; production was restricted to a limited number of firms holding licences to work. Looking back now, it seems difficult to imagine, but at that time it was against the law to make anything without holding the necessary permit. Fortunately, I did find a small firm that was willing to take me on as an apprentice cabinetmaker, and I can remember the great excitement of seeing furniture being made and some finished oak pieces 'in the white' – their natural state. The smell of freshly worked wood also made a great impression on me when I went for the interview. It was agreed that I would start work at the princely sum of 12/6d (62½p) per week.

The firm I worked for was owned by a Mr Cakebread, certainly the wrong name for a furniture maker. We produced handmade, machine-assisted, semi-reproduction furniture, the range being greatly restricted by the work licence held. Only pieces of a limited size and for a particular use could be made, such as small coffee tables or cabinets. These rules had to be strictly adhered to; if not, heavy fines could be levied against the firm. Once the war was over, however, the restrictions were gradually eased.

For the first two years of my apprenticeship my tasks were very mundane and extremely repetitive. Although it was a slow way of learning, it did instil a lot of discipline in the standard of my work, and it was a very good way of gaining the necessary hand skills.

The firm was housed in three main areas: one where the furniture was made, a polishing shop, and a machine shop. The machine shop was where I saw my first woodturning lathe. It was an enormous, enthralling monster, and I was completely fascinated by the sight of it being used; the noise, the shavings flying and the magic way in which square pieces of wood were quickly changed into quite complex, decorative *round* pieces. The lathe was driven by a DC electric motor, as were many machines in those days. These motors were massive when compared with the AC motors of today, and this particular example was situated on the floor in the corner of the workshop. A long, unguarded, 3in (76mm) wide canvas belt travelled upwards from the motor and drove a layshaft that ran across the workshop just under the ceiling. At one time it had probably been used to drive more than one machine. Another 3in (76mm) belt ran down from the layshaft to drive the headstock of the lathe. A stepped wooden pulley on the shaft, and another stepped in the opposite direction on the headstock, provided the gearing.

Each canvas belt was held together by a steel clip, but every now and again one of these clips would pull apart, causing the belt to fly off across the workshop. The belt on the headstock was always left very loose so that the operator could change the speed of the lathe while it was running, using a piece of wood to nudge the belt onto alternative top and bottom pulleys. Nobody ever seemed to clear up around this lathe, and to this day I do not know what was supporting the machine – for all I know, it could have been resting on a pile of shavings!

There was a window behind the lathe, but you would never have known that unless the sun shone, when the pile of wood dust that covered the window became a little lighter in colour than its surroundings. Everything around the lathe was caked in thick dust and shavings, which billowed up in great clouds when the machine was set in motion; when the belt became disconnected, a dense fog would occur in the lathe's vicinity.

The headstock and tailstock of the lathe were made from cast iron, but they were very crude castings. Each bearing was just a round piece of metal running through another piece of metal. On top of these were oil holders, which fed oil to the bearings to prevent them from overheating. If they were not kept filled with oil, the shaft would seize without warning, the lathe coming to an abrupt halt, and the belt snapping and flying off. The oil would drip from the bearings, splattering everywhere, including all over the operator and the workpiece.

The starter for the lathe was an open slide type, a large lever being moved to gradually build up the speed of the motor. Spectacular showers of sparks would issue from the starter, and I found it very frightening at first. The lathe would begin to turn slowly, but gradually increased speed, and as it did so the canvas belt would flap about, making an awful noise. As the craftsman began cutting the square section of wood, the shavings flew off as it took on its new shape. It was so quick. The work and the new shapes that evolved fascinated me.

We were making oak furniture at that time, and we used the lathe mostly to turn legs for tables, but also columns for buffets, and knobs for drawers and doors. Sometimes, wooden blanks were glued up with Scotch glue, to make them large enough for the legs of reproduction Tudor-style tables and buffets, which we often made. Occasionally, the joints would come apart, sending pieces of wood flying. This also greatly disturbed the dust.

The chisels and gouges we used were very crudely handmade by a blacksmith, and their handles were made from roughly shaped pieces of wood, more square than round. These handles were simply knocked onto the tools, without ferrules, and invariably they split. When this happened, a new piece of wood was quickly shaped and hammered on. Turned handles were the exception, not the rule. Looking back, I think the reason must have been that the rough handles were supposed to be a temporary measure, until someone got around to making proper ones, though no one ever did.

Other machines in this shop were even more dangerous than the lathe. We had a bandsaw that was potentially lethal, the blade being completely unguarded. Once, the blade broke and wrapped itself around the neck of a man nearby; fortunately, his injuries were only minor – some small cuts and scratches. There was a spindle moulder that had single blades in it, making it totally unbalanced and always in imminent danger of sending projectiles bullet-like across the workshop. On one occasion a blade actually flew past my ear. I did not realize what it was at first, but when I found out I became extremely wary of this machine. The factory inspectors of today would have had a field day in that machine shop.

An impatient wait

When I began my apprenticeship, I wanted to know everything about woodwork and the processes involved in furniture making. Fortunately, the experience I gained was very comprehensive. Apart from hand jointing and finishing, I learned to carve many of the traditional patterns. I was not allowed to use the machinery until I was 16, so I had to wait until then before I had my first experience of woodturning. By then, I was quite impatient to get to grips with the equipment, as I was very envious of the more experienced men who could rapidly turn quite complex shapes from square sections of wood. I could not wait for the mysteries of the machines to unfold for me.

In those days, much knowledge was gained by watching others and asking questions. When it came to my initial attempt at turning, I was given some brief instructions and left to turn a stool leg. Of course, this was one of the best stool legs ever made! The trouble came when I tried to make the set – I can remember making quite a number of different-shaped spares!

After another couple of years, my boss allowed me to work late at night making furniture for myself. This was very generous, but I now realize that it was also of benefit to him because I gained a lot of experience. This made me more confident in the various techniques that have proved very beneficial to me over the years. While working for myself in the evenings, I did a certain amount of turning. Apart from the legs for two tables and a stool, I also turned some small lidded bowls and a pair of tiered cakestands. I hate to imagine what the standard of the turning was.

I served my apprenticeship, like many others in those days, between the time I left school and the time I was called up to do my national service. It was late in 1950 that I received my call-up notice, which was followed by a medical. In the following January I joined the Royal Air Force and was posted to Wilmslow near Manchester, where I did my initial training. Despite my experience as a cabinetmaker, the RAF, in their wisdom, decided to train me to be an aircraft engine mechanic. Actually, I was very lucky, because most of the trade jobs were given to the enlisted men; most of my fellow conscripts were not given a trade, but were transferred to the RAF Regiment, which was virtually the same as being in the army.

Soon after I joined the RAF, my mother had to go into hospital for an operation and was seriously ill for a time. We had always been great friends and I did not really want to go too far away from her, especially while she was so ill.

In those days, there were various troubles all over the world: Mao was taking over China; there was an uprising in Malaya; there was trouble between the newly created state of Israel and the Arabs; not forgetting the unstable situation in Cyprus. However, there was a general feeling among us conscripts that if you volunteered for an overseas posting you would not get it. Well, that is what I thought, and if I did not get sent overseas, at least I could say that I had volunteered for it.

There were about 100 men in our training flight, and one evening towards the end of our training 15 of us were called out on the parade square in front of the others. First, one was told that he was going to Gibraltar and then dismissed to return to the rest of the flight. Others were told that they were off to Germany; five or six were being posted to the Middle East. This left me standing alone in front of all the rest. Thoughts raced through my mind: 'What about me? Where are they going to send me, and who with?' Then the sergeant uttered: 'Marsh, you are going to the Far East.'

I did not even think about the troubles out there. There was no one else with me. I was going all that way on my own. I did not know whether to cry my eyes out or what to do. Some of my mates said 'hard luck', while others said that it would be an experience. No one really seemed to be very jealous of me though. When I went home on leave and told my mother, she was great. Although she was still ill and I did not really want to leave her at that time, she told me to go, saying that it was 'a chance in a lifetime'.

After training, a short time in a transit camp and a brief spell of leave, I was flown to the Far East. After a five-day journey, I landed at Changi airport on the island of Singapore. From there, I was moved to Air Force Base Seletar. This is where I did my trade training to become an engine mechanic. When this was completed, I was transferred to a squadron, where first I worked on the engines of Spitfires, and later Mosquitoes and Hornets. This squadron's main purpose was to acclimatize newly trained pilots from England to the conditions in Malaya. They were being used as a strike force against the revolutionaries in the Malayan jungle. For me, it meant spending some of the time on the island of Singapore, and the rest on the mainland of Malaya at an air station called Butterworth, which was just on the edge of the jungle. That was a very frightening place, not only because of the bandits, but also because of the wildlife – snakes often slithered around our huts and made their homes in the roofs. The revolutionaries would often fire at us across the short stretch of water that separated Singapore from the mainland. This regularly occurred at night while we were on guard duty, protecting a squadron of flying boats.

Fig 1.4
On national service with the RAF in Malaya in 1951. Despite my cabinetmaking skills, I was trained as an engine fitter and worked on Spitfires, Mosquitoes and Hornets.

Fig 1.5
Under the wing of one of the Hornet fighters which I regularly serviced.

Looking back on my national service, I have some very happy memories. It gave me the opportunity to see and do many things that would never have been possible otherwise; I formed a number of lasting friendships, and the sense of comradeship stands out in my mind. It was quite an experience, and if I was asked whether or not I enjoyed it, the answer would have to be yes, given that I had no choice in the matter. It was a situation that I had to accept and make the most of. Memories always seem to dim the unpleasant aspects of life and to amplify the good. I was not overenamoured with my loss of freedom, the inability to make my own choices and the sometimes excessively regimental discipline. However, working on aircraft engines was very interesting, although there were times when I hankered to get back and work with wood. This was often the case when I saw the airframe fitters repairing the damaged parts of Mosquito aeroplanes, which were built of wood.

Just before Christmas 1952 I was flown back to England and billeted in a camp near Blackpool, to await my demobilization. This came as quite a shock, for we landed in the midst of a snow storm, which heralded one of our worst winters. On more than one occasion I longed to be back in the warmth of Singapore. Still, it would be Christmas at home, a short break and back to making furniture – or so I thought.

Starting afresh

When you were conscripted for national service, your employer had to guarantee your old job for at least six months on your return to civilian life. However, while I was away Mr Cakebread had got into financial difficulties and had gone bankrupt. There was no contingency plan for events like this, so I had no option but to look for another job.

When I left school, at the beginning of the summer holiday, I had applied for a job with a cabinetmaker named Dave Cohen. However, I could not start work until I was 14, and my birthday was not until the end of the holiday. Mr Cohen said that he was not willing to wait that long for me, so I got a job with Mr Cakebread instead, whose workshop happened to be next door. While I was serving my apprenticeship, Dave Cohen's son, Jack, left the army and set himself up in business making furniture. Mr Cakebread had expanded into larger premises, and he let Jack share the workshop in which I was working, so we got to know each other well. As Jack's business grew, I began to do his wood carving in the evening, after my normal day's work, which enabled me to earn some extra money.

By the time I had finished my national service, Jack Cohen's business had grown dramatically into Jaycee, which at the time produced hand-carved oak furniture (it is now owned by one of the major UK furniture manufacturers). On my return to civilian life he offered me a job carving, which I accepted, albeit with strong reservations. Apart from the fact that I did not want to do carving full-time, the business had grown and the other employees called him 'boss' or 'sir'. I still knew him as Jack, however, and often addressed him as such, which did not go down very well, particularly with one old carver I worked with. After two years in the RAF, I had had enough of calling people sir. Whereas I had become Mr Cakebread's right-hand man, concentrating on making one-off special pieces of furniture, with Jack Cohen I was back at the

Fig 1.6
Me aged 23, the year I got married.

bottom. The type of carving I was doing became very boring because there was only a limited number of designs, so the work was very repetitive.

In the RAF I had become aware that there was a great big world out there, and on leaving the service I found it difficult at first to settle back into civilian life. As a result, I only worked for Jack Cohen for a few weeks, leaving amicably by mutual consent. Directly after this, I got a job with a coachbuilder – there were still no jobs available making furniture. This company built wooden bodies for vans. Beginning with a factory-provided under-structure (engine, wheels, etc), we made the complete wooded cab and rear bodywork. I found this very interesting, as it was quite a different type of woodwork to that which I had been used to: the hand skills were very similar, but the processes and the end product were completely different.

My life as a coachbuilder lasted for about eight months; I left not because I was unhappy working there, but because I was offered more money to work for a company called Brighton Cabinets. The main attraction for making the move, though, was to get back to making furniture, but the money did add a small extra incentive.

Unfortunately, my time at Brighton Cabinets turned out to be one of my less happy periods of employment. I had been engaged to construct the proto-types of their designs, being responsible for the way in which each piece was constructed. This was a very interesting job to begin with, but as time went by the job changed, and I was required to find the cheapest way of producing the pieces, constantly having to cut corners. As a result, the bosses and I had a few disagreements. As the firm expanded, space in the workshop was at a premium, and a large belt sander without any dust extractor was sited very near to where I was working. This proved to be the last straw. I walked out in great haste, covered in sanding dust.

I then went to work for a high-class antique furniture shop that not only sold antiques, but also offered an interior design service, which could involve the complete furnishing of houses and flats. During this time, I made a lot of fitted furniture, ranging from single units to complete schemes for rooms and often whole houses. We also repaired a lot of antiques, and in many cases carried out complete renovation, or cut down and adapted pieces to make them more saleable.

It is fascinating how tastes change. In 1952 people seemed to want burr walnut finished furniture. We would buy in antique serpentine and bow-fronted chests and also writing desks, which were veneered in ebony, often having highly decorative inlaid patterns and very ornate decorated brass mounts. We would strip off all the ebony veneer and re-veneer them with burr walnut. Looking back on this, it was pure sacrilege; the original pieces would be extremely valuable now. I stayed at this company for about two years, working my way up to become foreman. Then, out of the blue, the owner closed the workshop.

Next, I moved to Jordan & Cook, a large retail furniture company in Brighton, where the work was very similar in many ways: making custom-built fitted furniture, many one-off freestanding pieces, repairing customer's furniture, and restoring antiques. It was an exciting job, made all the more interesting by the well-to-do clientèle, whose commissions provided the opportunity to make some delightful pieces of furniture. I spent ten years working for this company, finding the job both enjoyable and very satisfying. During my time there, I married my wife Mary, and my two sons, John and Peter, were born, but sadly my mother died.

The company experienced some financial difficulties, which were caused by the heavy duties levied after the death of the managing director. As a result, the shop premises, which included the workshop, were sold, and we moved to much smaller premises. The number of people employed was greatly reduced, and I felt that the situation was becoming rather insecure, so I looked around for another job, making furniture. However, things were to work out rather differently.

City and Guilds

When I was in the RAF, I had a conversation with a fellow conscript about what we had done in civilian life. He had been an electrician, and when I said that I was a cabinetmaker, he asked if I had my City and Guilds. I told him that I did not (if I had been honest, I would have said that I did not even know what they were), and he said that I could not be a cabinetmaker without them, which of course was not true, but that was how the conversation went. During my time in the RAF, I attended several education courses, and just prior to leaving I passed the necessary trade test to become a senior aircraftsman. This had taught me that while practical skills were essential, knowing the theory of a subject was very important too.

It was during my settled employment at Jordan & Cook that I learned of Brighton College of Art's intention to start running a City and Guilds cabinetmaking course. Curiosity led me to make enquiries and, as a result, in 1956 I enrolled for it. The course was due to run for four years, with atten-dance on three evenings a week. Ernest Joyce was in charge of the course, and I know that he was very impressed with my cabinetmaking skills which, not surprisingly, were more than competent by then. The result was that I ended up helping to teach my fellow students practical skills.

During the City and Guilds course, I learned a lot about the theory of furniture making and the materials used. Most importantly, it made me ask questions, and the course provided me with many answers. One evening a week was spent in a drawing class, learning about scale drawings, perspective, and the various projections, the conic sections, the golden rectangle and so on. I achieved a greater appreciation of the relationships between lines, curves and light. After a year, I took the intermediate examination, and two years later I took the final examination. I gained a first class pass in both.

Passing the exams did not raise my status, but it did give me a sense of achievement and added confidence in what I was doing. The reason I had taken them was because I was inquisitive to learn more about my chosen profession. After these two examinations, I went on to gain a City and Guilds Full Technology Certificate in Cabinetmaking. This certificate gave me a qualification to teach, and after a while I began teaching evening classes. Being married with two young sons and a mortgage, I found the extra money sufficient incentive to take this step.

I was then offered a full-time teaching post at Brighton College of Art, so I left Jordan & Cook to take up the appointment. When I joined the college in 1965, Ernest Joyce was still in charge of the furniture department, although

Fig 1.7
At Brighton Polytechnic in 1978, just prior to my heart attack.

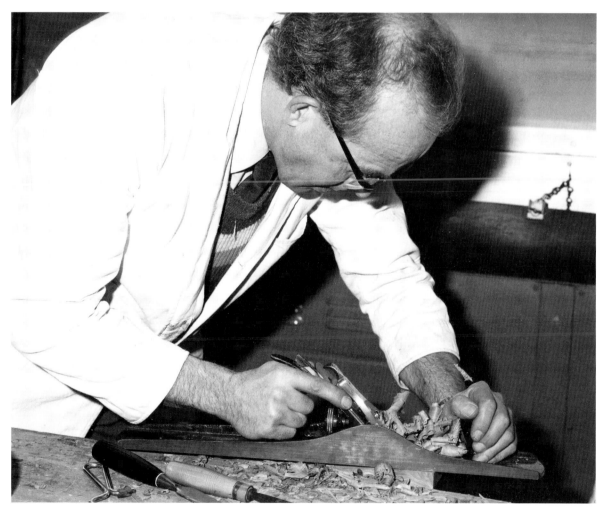

11

he was only employed on a part-time basis. Consequently, it was not long before I was taking considerable responsibility for the courses. In 1969 he retired, and I took over from him, being responsible for all the furniture courses. At that time, most of the courses were for day-release trade students, studying for their City and Guilds cabinetmaking examinations, but there were also evening classes for amateurs, and we held special classes for architects and art and craft teachers.

On taking over, I was also to initiate and run a new City and Guilds furniture-making course. This was a far more rounded course than cabinet-making, requiring the students to study upholstery, metalwork, plasticwork, wood machining, woodfinishing and other subjects related to furniture making. Soon after setting up this course, I was invited by the City and Guilds of London Institute to become one of their national assessors, and shortly after to become one of their examiners in both practical and theory subjects.

Gaining knowledge

My time teaching at the college was an extremely busy period of my life. Apart from teaching and preparing for lessons, there was the development and everyday running of the various courses, and the involvement with City and Guilds. Looking back now, I wonder how I also found time to improve my own knowledge about furniture making and the materials used.

Coincidentally, soon after I joined the college, I enrolled for a timber technology evening course at Brighton Technical College. The course was run by a friend of mine who talked me into enrolling, even though I thought I knew a lot about wood and could not see much to be gained from doing so. I soon realized how wrong I was. As time passed, my knowledge of wood became much deeper and my passion for the material grew. I joined the Sussex Wood Forum, a small group that organized lectures on wood and its many uses, and arranged visits to places of interest, including forests and plantations. As a result, I began to take an interest in the trees themselves.

After two years on the timber technology course, I passed the examination and was elected a member of the Institute of Wood Science. I found the course very satisfying indeed, the knowledge gained proving very useful in my newly chosen profession of teaching. It encouraged me to study even more. I set my sights on the Licentiateship of the City and Guilds of London Institute in Furniture Making, their highest award. To qualify for this, I needed to pass two of the three advanced examinations – Furniture Materials, Furniture Design and Furniture Production – and to show practical and responsible experience.

Studying for these examinations meant travelling to London two evenings a week, all at my own expense. Apart from the time spent travelling and attending the classes, a lot of personal home study had to be done. Each of these examinations was very involved, comprising several parts and topics. Between 1967 and 1970 I passed all three, with either a credit or a distinction. Subsequently, I was awarded my Licentiateship Certificate in Furniture Making.

Still not content, I carried on studying, again at evening classes, but fortunately nearer home at Worthing. This time, I studied machine woodworking, and by the end of 1972 I had passed the advanced craft examination and the three full technology qualifying examinations. This also led to my becoming a full member of the Institute of Wood Machine Technology, and eventually I was awarded the Licentiateship of City and Guilds in Wood Machining.

One ambition still remaining at that time was to study for and pass the Institute of Wood Science advanced examination. In 1978 I achieved this. It had meant attending Buckingham College of Higher Education for a number of study days, and much home study. To qualify meant sitting for two exami-nations and producing four in-depth study and research papers on certain chosen subjects: mine were wood preservation and wood finishing. I chose these because I found wood-boring insects and wood-attacking fungi quite fascinating.

None of these qualifications was taken with the thought of furthering my career, but rather because of my thirst for knowledge of wood and furniture making. Of course, I found all this study beneficial when I was teaching and also now in my career as a woodturner.

In 1971 Brighton College of Art joined with Brighton College of Technology to become Brighton Polytechnic, which led to many new degree courses being developed. One of these was in Wood, Metal, Ceramics and Plastics. The City and Guilds courses were transferred to the Technical College, but I stayed on at the Polytechnic to teach on the degree course, being one of the staff responsible for setting it up.

Struck down

In 1979, when I was 46 years old, my life was to change completely. I had a heart attack, which came as a great surprise, not only to myself and relatives, but to my colleagues at the college. Many regarded me as one of the fittest there, always rushing about and full of energy. Like so many people before, I did not realize what was happening. I had taken a morning off from the college, had got up early, taken some bags of rubbish to a nearby skip (the dustmen were on strike), and taken my youngest son to school. On my return home, I started working enthusiastically in my workshop, but suddenly I felt a slight restriction in my throat and began to feel increasingly hot; rushing upstairs for a drink of water made things worse. There was an incredible pain in my chest, which moved to my arms. As I lay rolling in agony, my wife telephoned the doctor who, on hearing how the pain had spread, soon had an ambulance on its way.

I spent the next five days in intensive care. As I lay there, I felt totally relaxed, probably the most relaxed I have felt in my life. I suppose this was due to the drugs that they had been giving me. Another five days followed on a normal ward. A heart attack is a very sobering event, making you realize that you are not indestructible. Being confronted by my own mortality made me think long and hard about my life. This was also brought sharply into focus when the doctor said: 'If you carry on smoking, you'll be gone before you're 60.' At first, this seemed a long

Fig 1.8
After my heart attack, I began turning again as therapy. Among the work I produced was this coopered bowl with hand-carved, pear-leaf motif. Pear, 10in (254mm) diameter, 3½in (89mm) high.

way off, but after a quick calculation with the aid of my fingers, I realized that life was not as long a process as I had once thought.

I returned to teaching for a time, but of course I was not completely fit, and gradually more pains developed in my chest. After various tests, it was decided that I needed open-heart surgery, but I had to wait for nearly two years before I had the operation. After a period of convalescence, I went back to teaching again, but I was still experiencing some pain, so after another 18 months I had a second operation. By now, after four years of illness, I was at a mental and physical low, and my doctors did not feel that I would be fit enough to continue teaching at the Polytechnic. If this had not been the case, I would probably never have made the decision to give up teaching and concentrate on woodturning.

Before this, I had never considered starting a business of my own, although teaching was beginning to lose some of its attraction. I had always enjoyed teaching and being involved with the students, and at times college life could be very satisfying and fulfilling, but the endless internal politics and the pointless meetings were incredibly frustrating.

Today, woodturning is the focus of my life and I would not change that situation, but when I look back at my decision to give up teaching and become a professional woodturner, it seems somewhat irresponsible. It may appear that one day I was a teacher, and the next I picked up a gouge to become a woodturner. But it was not like that at all. I had done some woodturning during my apprenticeship, which was mostly spindle turning using rather crude tools and equipment. On my return to civilian life after national service, there was no opportunity to do any turning at the firm where I worked, because any that was required would be sent out to a jobbing turner. The next woodturning I was to do was during my time as a student at Brighton College of Art, where I made a standard lamp, table lamps and various bowls.

While teaching at the college, I still had the urge to produce my own work, although there was little time to do so. Often, I found that turning a salad or fruit bowl after a day's teaching could be quite relaxing and satisfied my need to be creative. This work gradually became more complex and, of course, time consuming. Moving house in 1974 gave me the opportunity to set up my own workshop, and it was not long before I obtained my own

Fig 1.9
Just before my sabbatical, I made this bowl from 16 strips of ash, cut and rejoined with ebony veneers, and then coopered together. As well as being decorative, the brick-like structure is very strong. 10in (254mm) diameter, 3½in (89mm) high.

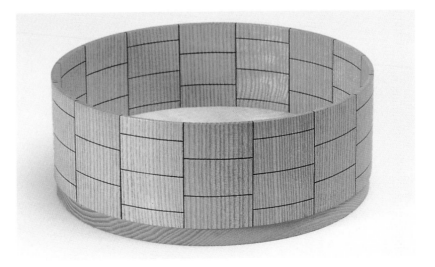

woodturning lathe, which allowed me to spend more time turning.

When the college became part of Brighton Polytechnic, some lecturers were offered a six-month sabbatical leave so that they could 'recharge their batteries' and carry out some kind of research that would be beneficial to them and their teaching. As time went by, I was asked to take such a sabbatical. Since I was the longest-serving member of our department, until I took my leave, no other member of the staff could take theirs.

I chose to study wood crafts in England and Denmark, and I planned to visit craftspeople, shops and galleries in both countries. In addition, I decided to spend time designing and making a number of turned wooden bowls. For several years, I had been working on ideas for bowls that involved building them up from small sections of wood, thus overcoming the long drying times necessary when using thick pieces of wood. Small-section wood was also more readily available, and often cheaper, than thick wood, and it was likely to have fewer faults.

Some of the bowls were made up from strips of wood like barrels, the grain running vertically from top to bottom, while others were turned from thick blocks made by laminating several thin strips together (see Figs 1.9 and 1.10). I also made large bowls by joining together sections of smaller bowls and then re-turning them.

During the year before my sabbatical I had spent much time developing these ideas, and I hoped to carry on and refine them during my study leave. At the culmination of my sabbatical, I intended staging an exhibition in the Polytechnic's gallery. I felt the need to justify my time away from teaching and I wanted to produce a good, comprehensive exhibition of woodturning, which would demonstrate the results of the techniques on which I had been working.

Fig 1.10
A spiral laminated bowl with separate base, made in 1979. Yew with two rosewood and one sycamore veneer glued on. 11in (279mm), 4in (102mm) high.

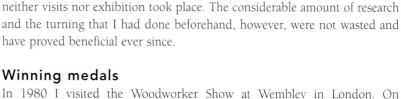

Shortly before my sabbatical was due to start, I had my heart attack, so neither visits nor exhibition took place. The considerable amount of research and the turning that I had done beforehand, however, were not wasted and have proved beneficial ever since.

Winning medals

In 1980 I visited the Woodworker Show at Wembley in London. On examining the various competition exhibits, and in particular the woodturning, I felt that I could compete. So in the following year, I entered four pieces, winning two gold medals and two silver medals (*see* Figs 1.11 and 1.12). I also won the overall award for the best piece of woodturning at the show. In the subsequent two years, I entered the woodturning competition again and was equally successful (*see* Figs 1.13, 1.14 and 1.15).

Before leaving the college, in most cases I had only exhibited single pieces and small groups of my woodturning. However, in 1982 I had exhibited 40 bowls at a gallery in Ashby-de-la-Zouch in Leicestershire, and 25 bowls at the art galleries of both Sussex and Southampton Universities. During my period of ill health and convalescence, I had occasionally managed to do some woodturning, which I found quite therapeutic.

Thus over the years, albeit unwittingly, I had laid the foundations for my future full-time profession. On leaving Brighton Polytechnic, I was obviously in a state of limbo for a while; I was mentally and physically very low, without any thought of what the future held for me. However, as time passed, I gradually built up my strength, and as this occurred I began to do more woodturning. The direction of my life became clearer and, of course, I developed a much more positive attitude.

Fig 1.11
Below **This bowl won the overall turning award at the 1981 Woodworker Show. The 12 sides were cut from six smaller bowls, then mitred and glued together before adding the separate base. Yew, 12in (305mm) diameter, 3in (76mm) high.**

Fig 1.12
Bottom **This shallow dish was turned with a very thin rim and has a separately turned hollow pedestal base. English yew, 10in (254mm) diameter, 2½in (64mm) high. Winner of a gold medal at the Woodworker Show, 1981.**

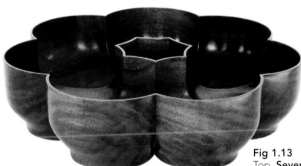

Fig 1.13
Top Seven small natural-edge vases made from the same laburnum log. These won a gold medal at the Woodworker Show, 1982.

Fig 1.14
Middle A walnut bowl made from seven smaller bowls, cut and joined together. 12in (305mm) diameter, 3½in (89mm) high. This bowl won the overall turning award at the Woodworker Show, 1982.

Fig 1.15
Bottom A pair of cherry bowls, each made from 16 turned segments, joined together and then a turned base added. 11in (279mm) diameter, 4in (102mm) high. Awarded a gold medal at the Woodworker Show, 1983.

Having assembled a collection of turned wooden objects, next came the difficulty of selling them. Luckily, this did not prove to be a serious problem. During my initial year as a professional woodturner, I sold my work locally in Sussex and was selected to become a member of the Sussex Guild of Craftsmen, and also a member of the British Crafts Centre (now the Contemporary Applied Arts). One exhibition of my work led to further invitations to exhibit at other venues. As time went by, I also visited galleries further afield to sell my work, having it accepted by the British Crafts Centre (*see* Fig 1.16), Casson Gallery and Innate Harmony Gallery – all of them in London. The Oxford Gallery, Oxford, and the Collection Gallery, Ledbury, also took pieces.

In 1984 I took part in my first craft fair, followed by others, and in October of that year I exhibited for the first time at Chelsea Crafts Fair. Useful contacts followed, and in 1985 I had a very busy programme of exhibitions, with major shows at Ombersley and St Albans, and others at Ditchling, Farnham and five venues in London. I had a one-man show in Blackburn, and to top it all, I was invited to have my own one-man major show at Hove Museum and Art Gallery (*see* Fig 1.17). This made me feel very proud indeed, Hove being where I spent my formative years.

Fig 1.16
This natural-edged elm vase was turned green and retains the bark on its rim. A similar vase was presented to the Queen of Tonga by the British Crafts Centre in 1983. Elm, 3½in (89mm) diameter, 3in (76mm) high.

Fig 1.17
A few of the bowls exhibited at Hove Museum and Art Gallery in the summer of 1985. In all, 132 pieces were put on show.

Since then I have had my work exhibited in many prestigious galleries throughout the world. Among the exhibitions of my work there have been a number of one-man shows, including a solo exhibition at the Barbican, London, in early 1995. Now I exhibit and sell my work not only all over the British Isles, but also in the USA, Canada, South Africa, Australia, Japan, Germany and several other countries.

Over the years, I have gained a very supportive clientele through these various events, shows and exhibitions, and my work has been purchased for a number of public collections and numerous private ones. I have also had the great honour of being made a fellow of the Designer Craftsmen and an honorary member of the Guild of Master Craftsmen. My work has also been accepted for the British Crafts Council Selected Index and my name has been entered in the Debretts Peerage publication, *People of Sussex*. I feel very fortunate to have had these honours bestowed upon me, especially as I am doing something that gives me great pleasure and enormous satisfaction.

Looking back, I often wonder what I would have been doing had I not encountered – and been enchanted by – that monster lathe during my cabinetmaking apprenticeship.

②Philosophy

From an early age, I have felt a profound need to work with wood; I love the material passionately. There is no complex philosophy attached to the work I do; I am simply striving to achieve the perfect form, the purest possible curves expressed in simple, uncluttered shapes that will expose the beauty of the wood to the full. In seeking that goal, I find inspiration in many everyday objects, but most of all I am inspired by the wood itself.

Although in my days as a furniture maker, turning had been a part of my job, when I took up teaching it became a means of relaxation and of satisfying the need I had to work with wood. Teaching allowed me little time to make furniture, but turning was instant; at the end of the day, in the quiet of the workshop, I could produce a bowl before going home. After my illness, I still had a desire to work with wood, but I had neither machinery, space nor even the strength to make furniture. Turning was much more convenient and quickly became the driving force in my life, fulfilling my need to be creative.

I have always found working with my hands to be easy, and I enjoy the techniques of working wood. It is easy to understand and an extremely rewarding material to work. There are frustrations, of course, because of its unpredictability, but that is what makes it exciting, and a lot of the joys and satisfaction of working it are derived from overcoming the causes of frustration.

Indeed, I cannot imagine doing anything but working in wood, which is why I needed to do some work for myself while I was teaching. I simply wanted to enjoy the sensations of working the material. There is enormous satisfaction in picking up a piece of timber and shaping it into something. I can get that satisfaction from planing, or sawing and making a piece of furniture, but turning on the lathe can result in a much more instant satisfaction.

Experiment to develop

Although I had turned a few bowls over the years, it was not until I was teaching at the college that I really began to develop bowl turning. I had my share of problems, and sometimes things flew around the workshop, but if something did go wrong, I made the effort to find out why and put it right so that it did not happen again. Mistakes are all part of the learning process. If you do not make them occasionally, you are probably not experimenting, and that means you are probably not developing. You need the frustration of failure to appreciate having really achieved something. Of course, if you do not learn by your mistakes, you might as well give up.

When I first began using a lathe, as an apprentice, most of the work I did was spindle turning – making legs and other parts for furniture – and my only aim was to make each piece match the others as closely as possible. The process of doing that was satisfaction in itself. Even then, though, I was thinking about shapes. We were making semi-reproduction styles of furniture and the parts had to be made exactly as specified. They were far from authentic antique shapes, and often I thought they should have been more like the originals they were copied from.

In those days, the shapes of most turned bowls – mine included – were unimaginative and crude. Each was simply an attempt at making as large a container as possible while wasting as little wood as possible. Consequently, they tended to be fairly oblong in section.

Having seen the work of ornamental turners, I wanted to produce more complex curves and shapes. I was impressed with what ornamental turners could do with wood – it still impresses me – but in reality I was admiring the technical skills of the makers and the ingenuity of their machines. The tedium of setting up their machines holds no attraction for me, but their work inspired me to try to make my bowls more interesting. I began producing bowls made up of sections, including turned sections; I inlaid and built up, but it was all technique, and the techniques were restricting the finished shape (*see* Fig 2.1). The work was like that of the ornamental turners – fiddly and heavily involved in how various elements could be worked together; how this could be joined to that; was it possible to do this? I was concentrating all the time on *how* to make the piece, not on *what* I was making.

Fig 2.1
Three dovetail grooves were turned in this 16-sided coopered bowl; then the sides were planed to give this scalloped look. Yew, 12in (305mm) diameter, 3½in (89mm) high.

A point of view

When you look at an object, what you see varies according to where you are in relation to the object and the object's relation to its surroundings. If you are looking up at something, you perceive it differently than if you are looking down on it, or if it is at eye level. Your perception of the object depends on its relationship to the textures and colours around it. Subtle lighting or bright lighting can 'lift' or 'lower' an object quite considerably.

I was having a lengthy discussion along these lines with an artist colleague of mine one day. We were talking about certain pieces of sculpture and eventually we turned to the subject of the relationship of an object to the ground. Before this time, I had always taken this for granted, never having thought about it or analysed it in any way. The realization that what an object was standing on, or where it was situated, could make an enormous difference to the way in which that object was perceived was a great step forward for me. Of course, the colours of the object and the surface on which it stands will have an effect, too. Most wooden pieces are brown, and they appear to settle into a dark surface, whereas on a light surface, they will be lifted up. The light, its direction and the formation of shadows all play a part in how we see things.

When you analyse the shapes of objects in relation to what they are standing on, they fall into three distinct categories (*see* Fig 2.2). There are those that look as if they have been constructed on the ground, or are simply laid on top of it. Most buildings fall within this group, and a prime example is the Parthenon. With this kind of shape, it appears that you could simply transport the object from one place to another without affecting the object itself or the ground on which it stands.

Fig 2.2
The three categories of shape.

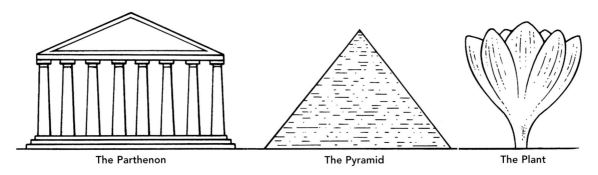

| The Parthenon | The Pyramid | The Plant |

Then there are objects that break through the surface, giving the impression that there is more underneath and that the further the object emerges, the bigger it becomes while retaining the same proportions as when it first started to break through the surface. The pyramids in Egypt are archetypal of this form.

The third category is where objects push through the ground and develop above it. Plants are like this, pushing up through the earth, continually developing upwards and outwards – living (*see* Figs 2.3 and 2.4). Today, I strive to achieve that form in my work (*see* Fig 2.5).

All the early bowls I made – or perhaps I should say constructed – fell into the first category. Initially, they were quite simple, but then I became interested in the idea of making bowls by joining several pieces of wood together. I developed this idea, becoming deeply involved in joining the various elements, and concentrating on the construction problems and the skills required to make the pieces well enough so that they would join together perfectly. The finished shape was almost incidental. When it was finished, my self-criticism tended to be aimed at the success of the construction and the craftsmanship involved in that construction. Occasionally, I did feel uneasy about the form, which was quite restricted, but I was proud of what I had achieved, and this overshadowed the aesthetic considerations. It was as if I was producing something for a technical examination, or a trade test, where you had to demonstrate as many different skills as possible on a test piece. The test piece is not supposed to be anything, or to look attractive; it merely demonstrates that you have mastered a particular set of skills. Shortly before I had my heart attack, I realized just how restrictive these techniques were and reverted to turning solid pieces of wood, much of it green (unseasoned).

A new range of influences

My attitude to what I was making changed when the college became a polytechnic, and I was introduced to a new range of influences. The course I was teaching on was extended to include metal, ceramics and plastics, as well as wood, and the department in which I was working became involved in pottery, silver, plastics and other materials. In the back of my mind, I had already begun considering form and the relationships of materials, but I had not specifically applied my thoughts to what I was doing with turning. I had tried to make bowls thinner, and different shapes, but it was still a subconscious process. Then I began to ask myself: 'Why the devil do we have to make a bowl that always tries to achieve the maximum storage area from any particular piece of wood?' So I experimented. I was one of the first people to make bowls that *lost* so much wood. I had started to move away from practical considerations, towards a more aesthetic type of turning.

By focusing on techniques, I had given little consideration to form. However, that period concentrating on technique was very useful, because it meant that I acquired the skills of turning that allow me so much more freedom now; I can achieve precisely the shapes I want without having to worry about how I am holding the gouge, because this is second nature to me. But this is not enough on its own. You need inspiration, then technique – which is the means to produce the shape you have in mind – and the material. The combination of all three should give you the result you are looking for. Only after the skills had become second nature did I feel able to experiment with form.

Although skills are essential to refine the pieces we make, they can also impose restrictions of their own, as can relying on the tried and tested methods you may have developed for doing things. They can discourage

Fig 2.3
Top **Crocuses breaking through the ground in the spring.**

Fig 2.4
Above **The flowers gradually opening out.**

Fig 2.5
Below **A trio of three spalted, beech-bark-edged vases (1983). These are typical of the small-based bowls I began to turn at about this time. 5in (127mm) diameter, 5–6in (127–152mm) high.**

experimentation, which results in a lack of fresh ideas. When other turners do things differently, it is always worth comparing their methods to your own. Keep an open mind, and never assume that your way will always be the best.

Inspiration is essential, but can be elusive. Without it, you can end up either with something that would have been better left as a piece of wood, or with a copy of another person's work. There is nothing wrong in being inspired by someone else's work, and even copying it as you develop, but the time should come when you take the next step forward, developing a style of your own with something of yourself in it.

Many turners still produce that basic 'building-type' shape. Having paid for a piece of wood, they want to end up with as little of it as possible as waste, so they turn off the corners and hollow it out, making the bowl as big as possible with little regard for the final form. But you have to ask yourself *why* you are making that bowl. If it is because you want to produce something beautiful, you have to forget the amount of wood that is removed and concentrate purely on the form. Of course, there will always be people for whom function is all, and who will never appreciate abstract beauty. They cannot see that a bowl might be desirable even though you can't put anything in it.

Pure curves

If a definition of 'art' is 'the creation of works of beauty exercising human skill', and beauty is in the eye of the beholder, then I suppose my work could be considered art. However, I regard myself as a craftsman, not an artist. My work has nothing in common with what seems to qualify these days as 'art'. I do not have a sophisticated 'philosophy', or any theories about it; I simply try to produce the purest possible curves that I can.

It seems to me that for something to qualify as art, it has to be complicated – involving theory – and my work does not fit in. It is pure and uncomplicated. I turn the pieces I make because I get extreme pleasure from the work, and from the result when I have exposed the beauty of the wood. I do not analyse what I do, or attach any intellectual theory to it, although I often analyse the finished pieces.

When you are learning the skills involved in woodturning, improving your techniques is important for your sense of achievement and satisfaction. Mastery of the techniques is essential if you are to create good work, and without a high degree of skill, your work will be limited. However, command of technique should not be seen as an end in itself; it is simply the means by which you can produce a beautiful bowl. Form is paramount.

I have become very competent technically (although I am learning all the time), and I need to be if I am to concentrate on the design of what I am making, rather than on how I am holding the gouge. Once you have perfected the groundwork, you can adapt and experiment with confidence.

The dilemma that faces every creative person who relies on their craft for their livelihood, is producing things that will sell, while still finding time to explore and extend their repertoire. You need time to make things because you *want* to make them, rather than thinking about what will sell. If you do not make this time to explore, your work becomes staid and restricted, and you do not progress.

When I set out to become a professional woodturner, if my work had not sold, I would have had a storage problem, and I would have had to find another way of earning a living. But I would still have gone on and produced a certain amount, because at that time I *needed* to make those bowls and develop my own style of turning.

I am always, always striving to achieve a perfect form – or, at least, something a little closer to it than anything I have done before. There is always further to go. Some turners may tell you otherwise: they will say that their work is marvellous and that they are satisfied with it. I believe that if you feel you have reached that stage, you might as well give up. You should always be aiming to improve. There are times when you get excited about a particular piece and you can even say that it is your best work yet, but if you are progressing, that particular piece might not even seem particularly good in a few years' time. When I look back at some of the pieces I have made, which I was proud of at the time, I realize that they were not good at all. I almost feel ashamed of some of them.

Development is a question of taking some steps forward and some back. You may make something that is nearly at your elusive best. You think you can just change a curve or the relationship of dimensions and it will be perfect, but when you change them on the next piece you find it is not as good as the one before. So you experiment some more and eventually you take the next step forward with a shape you like. Then you develop that. After a few steps, you look back at the first piece, which you thought was so good, and you can see it has marked a step in your development, but it does not look like such a big step anymore. Of course, when you look back on other work, you can see just how far you have moved on.

At one time I used colouring and texturing. I would carve bowls and scorch them and wire brush them. I made spiral bowls (*see* Fig 2.6) and others built up from turned pieces joined together. At this stage, I was at the extreme of being totally absorbed by technique, without being much concerned with form.

Fig 2.6
Spiral-laminated bowl with separate base (1978).
African walnut and sycamore,
11in (279mm) diameter,
4in (102mm) high.

Often, I may explore an idea by sketching it out on paper before I start to make the bowl. It may be only a few simple lines, no more than a doodle; it might be a silhouette. These are just two-dimensional ideas, and while they are starting points that work on paper, they often have to be changed when it comes to producing them in three dimensions. Say you have a 6in (152mm) piece of wood by 4in (102mm) deep, you can start with that shape on a sheet of paper and draw something that pleases you. So you start turning the bowl, adjusting the shape as you go. Then perhaps you will come across a split in the wood, or some other feature that you do not want to use, so you take it out. The design ends up very different from the one you first drew. In the end, the *wood* dictates to you what the bowl is going to look like.

So you have to be prepared to work *with* the wood, but you also have to take control of it. If the wood is such that you can only achieve a certain rim size, you have to be prepared to alter the relationship of the rest of the work to that size so that the overall piece is still well proportioned and balanced.

Appropriate shapes

When you start to think about form, you begin to question how appropriate wood is for certain shapes. For example, if you make platters, many people are not really aware of the shape. When they look down on a platter, they get excited about the wood and hardly notice the shape.

Some shapes are also more applicable to one material than another. Glass, for example, lends itself to closed vessels, or hollow forms as they are called in woodturning. This is partly because of the process of glass blowing, and partly because the transparency or opaqueness of the material allows you to see inside. I do not turn hollow forms because I do not think that wood lends itself to this form of expression. It is a waste because you cannot see the beauty of the wood on the inside through that little opening. I can appreciate the skills required, which can be quite considerable, and I admire many of the turners who make them, some of whom give serious consideration to the final

Fig 2.7
At one time I became so obsessed with form that I finished my work with black lacquer to conceal the grain. This bowl, made in 1985, is an example. It has a hollow pedestal base, turned separately. Brazilian mahogany, 11in (279mm) diameter, 6in (152mm) high.

form. I like some of the forms, too; they can have an air of mystery about them. But I want the inside of my work to be finished as well as the outside, and because of the small aperture you cannot get inside a hollow form to give it that fine finish.

Exploration of form led me to another realization: the look of the wood is not everything. A good piece of wood only makes a good bowl if the form of the bowl is right. You make a bowl out of a nice piece of wood and it is fresh and sparkling, but then the wood matures and it darkens, or lightens, which is something you have to accept with wood. As this happens, it loses its sparkle and becomes increasingly bland, which is why the shape is so important.

At one time, I became so engrossed with the idea of form being paramount that I finished some of the pieces I made with black lacquer (*see* Fig 2.7). I had become depressed watching people pick up my bowls, saying 'that's a nice piece of wood'. I thought that if they could not see anything in it except that it was a nice piece of wood, they might just as well buy an attractive piece of wood. By lacquering my work, I wanted to force them into seeing the form and appreciating it without looking at the wood. This also proved a good discipline for myself. At first I filled the grain before I lacquered it so the bowls lost the texture of the grain altogether, but I was not happy with this. I found the appearance of the bowls more pleasing when the grain showed, so I stopped filling it, although I was still staining and lacquering the wood. After a while, I also found the bowls less satisfying without the wood being exposed. In the end I realized that for someone to say 'what a lovely piece of wood' was not so insulting, because what I try to do is expose the beauty of that piece of wood. Now I see that when someone comments favourably on the quality of the wood, they are confirming that I have achieved that aim.

A new interest

By covering up the wood, I think I was giving myself a chance to explore form alone, without the distraction of the grain pattern. With that heightened awareness, I started looking at the things around me with a new interest.

Being visually aware is something we all have to work at. Many of the objects we see each day are taken for granted; so much so that often they do not consciously register in our minds. Although I had lived in Brighton all my life, it was only at this stage that I began to really *see* the domes of the Brighton Pavilion. There are more shapes up there than I had ever dreamed of, and I am still finding new ones (*see* Figs 2.8 and 2.9). I studied the work of potters and silversmiths, and absorbed those shapes. I looked at fences and roofs and fascias and gravestones; at fuchsias and tulips and roses and crocuses, all with a new awareness. And all these shapes went into my head as I developed an appreciation of form.

I must emphasize that when I say these shapes give me inspiration, that is exactly what I mean. I do not look at them and go away and reproduce them. I do not copy plants, or ceramic pots, or silverware bowls or anything else, but I am sure that certain shapes influence the forms I make, although this is a subconscious process. My work is the result of having studied all kinds of shapes that I see around me, and what I see forms part of the reserve of knowledge about form in my memory. Unless you put something into your

Fig 2.8
The domes of Brighton's Royal Pavilion. The variety of shapes up there is incredible, and I am still finding new ones.

Fig 2.9
Another view of the shapes on the roof of the Royal Pavilion.

Fig 2.10
Top Park railings around Princes
Park, Edinburgh. Railings such
as these form part of our
everyday environment and are
easily taken for granted, but
looking for the shapes in such
objects will help you to develop
an appreciation of form.

Fig 2.11
Above Shapes on the top of
some wrought-iron gates in a
Brighton park.

Fig 2.12
Right Even gravestones can
provide a wealth of shapes to
study.

brain, nothing is going to come out. But if you look at a shape and set your mind on copying it, you will fail. There can only be one original, but few people seem to realize that.

I bought a telephoto lens for my camera and I take pictures of rooftops and flowers and gravestones and railings – anything with an interesting form (*see* Figs 2.10, 2.11 and 2.12). I take photographs not so much because I want the finished prints, but because when you are taking a photograph, you have to look through the viewfinder and concentrate your mind on that particular subject. It forces you to be observant. I do look at the photographs after they have been processed, but they are soon filed away and I rarely look at them again. However, taking the photograph has reinforced the image in my brain and, I hope, is also an aid to my becoming ever more visually aware.

I do not only take photographs of objects I like. I also take pictures of things I find ugly, but for the same reason – to help me analyse the shape and understand why it does not work (for me, at least). The whole process makes me more discerning and that, I hope, shows in my work.

Sometimes I look at something and wonder what its inspiration was. The Brighton Corn Exchange, for example. It is part of the Brighton Pavilion complex, and above the entrance is a castellated parapet. Each castellation has certain similarities to a gravestone (*see* Fig 2.13). So was the architect inspired by gravestones? Or perhaps gravestones were inspired by the castellation? Then again, the different craftsmen could have been feeding off each other, the architect being inspired by the gravestones, then the monumental mason being influenced by the parapet.

Rooftops and skylines are interesting subjects for photography. Against the plain background of the sky, the shape itself becomes clear. These shapes can become even clearer in a photograph (*see* Fig 2.14). A black silhouette against a bright sky produces a pure form, no longer complicated by colour and texture. Edinburgh, Oxford, Cambridge, York, as well as Brighton and many other places have all provided me with fascinating and exciting subjects to photograph.

Sometimes, a particular object or part of an object can form the focus of my attention. On other occasions, the whole skyline provides an array of juxtaposed forms. The exercise of taking these photographs has been instrumental in developing my sense of form and scale, and enhancing my appreciation of aesthetics.

Fig 2.13
Above left **What was the inspiration behind these castellations on the Brighton Corn Exchange? Gravestones perhaps?**

Fig 2.14
Above right **Royal Pavilion shapes in sillhouette.**

Fig 2.15
This trophy was commissioned for the 'Woodturner of the Year' competition, and was made in one piece. Cocobolo, 3½in (89mm) diameter, 8in (203mm) high (1992).

What looks good

When I am working on the lathe, I use the combination of all the information that I have put into my brain to produce curves that satisfy me. Although I have learned the rules of design, I do not measure my pieces. I produce what looks good, and I do not know if they fulfil the conditions of the golden section or not – I just know when they look right. And if they do not look right, I reject them. I might have finished the outside of a bowl completely before I know that the shape is wrong. If it is, I will change it and refinish the bowl or, if necessary, throw it away.

I have a passion for perfection. It is a funny sort of attitude and it is contrary really, because I am using a material that has so many characteristics that frustrate attempts at perfection. It cracks and splits and is always moving, but it is the material I have chosen to use and which I love passionately, perhaps even *because* it is unpredictable.

Mounting a piece of wood on the lathe is the start of a voyage of discovery, and some of those voyages are more significant than others. There is the mystique of what you will make from it and what you will discover within it. It is strange how those important voyages of discovery start out. I was once commissioned to make a trophy for a woodturning competition, and there were certain constraints in terms of its size, the wood used and the price, but I found that challenging, and the trophy I produced was aesthetically very pleasing. In accomplishing the brief, I found the voyage unexpectedly interesting (*see* Fig 2.15).

Although I love wood, I sometimes envy the craftsmen who work in clay and glass because of the plasticity of those materials. They can make something and then push it sideways, or pull a piece out, or whatever. Sometimes, I wish wood had the properties of other materials, but that is just looking for greener grass. I am sure a lot of craftspeople occasionally look to the materials of others with envy, but in the end each medium has its own properties, and I am happy to accept wood the way it is.

Fig 2.16
Commissions can often
produce an interesting
challenge. This bowl was
presented to Howard Davies
of the CBI, who was voted
'Communicator of the Year' in
an award scheme sponsored
by Digital Equipment. Burr
elm, 13in (330mm) diameter,
8in (203mm) high (1992).

Bert Marsh Woodturner

When I want to escape the regularity in the finished work imposed by a lathe, I turn green wood and natural-edged pieces (*see* Fig 2.17). Green wood distorts appreciably as it dries, losing its smooth regularity. To a certain extent, the distortion is predictable, and it can be partially controlled by putting on a finish while the wood is still wet – which slows down the drying process and limits the level of distortion – or by turning it so that the grain runs in a particular direction to create distortions in that way. But whatever measures you take, there is always some element of surprise in what the wood will do.

Fig 2.17
Green-turned burr elm vase with a natural edge (1992). As this vase dried it became quite textured and the top edge became wavy. 8in (203mm) diameter, 6in (152mm) high.

Fig 2.18
Burr jarrah vase, turned semi-
dry (1990). A slightly textured
surface developed on this
vase. 11in (279mm) diameter,
8in (203mm) high.

For the future, I want to continue to explore shapes in my work, but
that is not to say I want to make any major changes to the way I work, or what
I make. The process is one of careful refinement. If I was to change my work
radically, I would have to change my philosophy and rethink my reasons for
doing what I am doing. I want to continue to make simple, uncluttered shapes
(see Fig 2.18). I do not like grooves, or flutes or any surface decoration that
spoils the overall shape. I just want those curves to flow.

Basically, I like to do justice to each piece of wood and show it to its best
advantage, as far as my skills and knowledge will allow. That is the greatest
satisfaction I get, and the greatest challenge, because you can never reach the
perfection you are striving for.

I cannot say exactly where my work is going; if I could, there would be
no point in making those voyages of discovery to get there.

Gallery One

The vessels featured in this gallery are a selection of my work since becoming a professional woodturner. They are a diverse group of bowls and vases, using many different types of wood, each one with its own specific character.

Some of the pieces have regular top rims, whilst others use the natural shape of the log for their top edge. In certain cases the bark is used to add extra detail. Freshly felled wood has been used, full of moisture, and has been turned and finished completely before leaving the vessel to dry naturally, causing distortion in the piece and a texturing of the surface.

Dry wood has also been used, and in such cases the bowl or vase was often rough turned, allowing a further drying period of a year or even more, before the final turning and finishing was carried out.

The thickness of the walls varies slightly depending on the type of wood used and the size of the vessel. Average thickness is $\frac{1}{2}$in (2mm).

Approximate dates when made are given in brackets.

Laburnum vase (1983). Natural edge, turned dry. This could be considered my signature piece. The vase was turned from a small log, the heart of which lies across the vase. A strong contrast between the heartwood and the sapwood is evident. 5½in (140mm) diameter, 5½in (140mm) high.

Above
Spalted sycamore vase (1985).
Turned dry and rough turned.
The foot of the vase has been
turned hollow. 8in (203mm)
diameter, 5in (127mm) high.

Opposite
Holm oak vase (1986). Bark
edge, turned green. The dark
bark edge is in very striking
contrast to the light-coloured,
textured wood. 7½in (191mm)
diameter, 7in (178mm) high.

Right
Yew bowl (1986). Turned dry.
This was made from half a log
with the heart at the top rim.
It has no foot and is
completely rounded over. 13in
(330mm) diameter, 5½in
(140mm) high.

Below
Ziricote vase (1987). Natural
edge, turned dry. There is a
sharp contrast between the
creamy grey sapwood rim and
the dark, greenish black,
highly figured heartwood.
4½in (114mm) diameter, 5in
(127mm) high.

Spalted beech vase (1987).
Turned dry. A very decorative
vase due to the striking black
zone lines of the fungal attack
in the wood. 4½in (114mm)
diameter, 4½in (114mm) high.

Sumach vase (1988). Bark
edge, turned green. This was
made from one of the
casualties of the 1987 storm.
6in (152mm) diameter, 4½in
(114mm) high.

Spalted beech vase (1988). Turned dry. A highly decorative vase due to the spalting of this usually bland timber. 11in (279mm) diameter, 5½in (140mm) high.

Above
Laburnum vase (1989). Natural
edge, turned dry. The three
hearts are due to the vase
having been turned from part
of a log which had forked into
two. 7¼in (184mm) diameter,
6in (152mm) high.

Opposite
Mulberry vase (1989). Bark
edge, turned green. The heart
runs straight across the centre
of the vase with light sapwood
below the bark and around
the foot, giving a pleasing
contrast to the golden
heartwood. 7½in (190mm)
diameter, 7in (178mm) high.

Top
Spalted elm vase (1990).
Turned dry and rough turned.
The heart of the log is
positioned in the centre of the
top rim. Fungus zone lines
radiate away from it, and
strong black patches extend
to the foot of the vase. 14in
(356mm) diameter, 6¾in
(171mm) high.

Bottom
Burr jarrah bowl (1990).
Turned semi-dry. A slightly
textured surface developed on
this exceptional piece of burr
jarrah. 9½in (241mm) diameter,
5½in (140mm) high.

Opposite
Burr jarrah vase (1990).
Natural edge, turned green.
The greyish sapwood around
the top edge contrasts with
the deep reddish brown of the
heartwood. As the wood
dried, the surface developed a
very pleasing texture. 4in
(102mm) diameter, 5½in
(140mm) high.

Above
Burr jarrah vase (1991). Turned
dry after rough turning. This
simple form is highlighted by
a strikingly coloured wood.
11in (279mm) diameter, 6in
(152mm) high.

Opposite
Holly vase (1991). Bark edge,
turned green. As this vase
dried the heart across the
centre distorted the form,
giving the vase a lovely oval
shape. 6in (152mm) diameter,
5½in (140mm) high.

Spalted burr horse chestnut vase (1992). Turned dry. Vivid zone lines caused by the fungi which attacked the wood while it was still growing, make this bland wood highly decorative. 5½in (140mm) diameter, 3½in (89mm) high.

African blackwood vase
(1992). Natural edge, turned
dry. The sharp contrast
between the creamy sapwood
and the black heartwood,
make this piece very striking.
4½in (114mm) diameter, 6½in
(165mm) high.

Above
Burr jarrah vase (1992). Turned
dry. The honeycombing
developed as the burr dried,
giving this piece an open
lattice effect. 7½in (190mm)
diameter, 5in (127mm) high.

Opposite top
Burr maple vase (1992).
Natural edge, turned green.
The surface became quite
textured after final drying.
4¾in (121mm) diameter, 5¼in
(133mm) high.

Opposite bottom
Burr maple vase (1992).
Natural edge, turned green.
11in (279mm) diameter, 5½in
(140mm) high.

Opposite
Sycamore vase (1993). Turned dry and rough turned. Due to the lack of pigment within this wood, the vase is translucent. 11in (279mm) diameter, 5¼in (133mm) high.

Left
Ziricote vase (1993). Turned dry after rough turning. This striking wood makes the vase a very decorative piece. 8½in (216mm) diameter, 3in (76mm) high.

Below
Ziricote vase (1994). Turned dry after rough turning. The two amorphous patches of light sapwood give a striking contrast to the dark, figured heartwood. 4in (102mm) diameter, 4in (102mm) high.

Opposite
Ziricote vase (1994). Turned dry after rough turning. The black line figuring makes this piece highly decorative. 4in (102mm) diameter, 4in (102mm) high.

Opposite top
Cocobolo vase (1994). Turned dry after rough turning. This wood always produces a highly decorative piece. 4in (102mm) diameter, 2in (51mm) high.

Opposite bottom
Cocobolo vase (1994). Turned dry after rough turning. 5in (127mm) diameter, 2in (51mm) high.

Left
African ebony vase (1994). Turned dry after rough turning. This nearly black wood shows the form of the vase to best effect. 4½in (114mm) diameter, 2½in (64mm) high.

Above
Laburnum vase (1994). Bark
edge, turned green. The bark
causes a further contrast to
the sapwood and the
heartwood. As this piece
dried, the bark became wavy.
6½in (165mm) diameter, 3½in
(89mm) high.

Right
Burr elm vase (1994). Natural
edge, turned green. There is a
sharp contrast between the
creamy sapwood and the
warm brown, figured
heartwood; the surface has a
pleasing texture. 9in (229mm)
diameter, 4½in (114mm) high.

Opposite
Olivewood vase (1995).
Natural edge. Turned from a
complete round log, the heart
extends across the centre of
the vase. 10in (254mm)
diameter, 6½in (165mm) high.

Cocobolo box (1990). The
shape of this box makes it
very pleasant to hold and to
feel. 2½in (64mm) high, 2in
(51mm) diameter.

Olivewood box (1990).
The concave surface of the top of
the lid emphasizes the decorative
qualities of this wood. 2½in (64mm) high,
2in (51mm) diameter.

Palmwood box (1990). The
wood for this box is often
known as porcupine wood,
because of its appearance.
2½in (64mm) high, 2in (51mm)
diameter.

Honduras rosewood box
(1991). The flash of sapwood
makes a stunning feature of
this box. 2½in (64mm) high,
3in (76mm) diameter.

Cocobolo box (1991). To me cocobolo is the most decorative of all the rosewoods, each piece having a character of its own. 2½in (64mm) high, 3in (76mm) diameter.

Olivewood box (1991). Pieces
made from olivewood are
always very decorative due to
the many colours within it.
2½in (64mm) high, 3in (76mm)
diameter.

Burr elm box (1991). The
knots and the irregular grain,
as well as the colour, greatly
add to the interest of the
piece. 2½in (64mm) high, 3in
(76mm) diameter.

Spalted burr horse chestnut box (1992). Horse chestnut is normally a very bland and uninteresting wood. The piece used for this particular box is quite different; the dark zone lines and the various colours caused by the fungal attack, as well as the knots of the burring, make this an exceptional box. 2½in (64mm) high, 3in (76mm) diameter.

Right
Ziricote box (1993). The convex shape of the lid shows the striking black figuring of this wood at its best. 2½in high, 3in (76mm) diameter.

Opposite
African blackwood box (1993). This nearly black wood with its purple tinge is very hard indeed. Due to its close texture, a very fine surface finish can be achieved. 2½in (64mm) high, 3in (76mm) diameter.

③Timber

Understanding wood is an important part of being able to work it successfully, and the more I have found out about it, the more I have come to appreciate and admire it. It is a unique, sometimes frustrating, material with wide variations in density, texture, grain pattern and colour that provide a deep natural beauty. All these aspects can be used to good effect when turning bowls.

From my earliest days – certainly long before I left school – wood held a great fascination for me, and by the time I turned to teaching the subject, I thought I knew a lot about it. Then I attended a timber technology course and discovered just how little I really knew. From that moment, I developed a greater interest in wood and spent a lot of time studying the mysteries of the material. Even now, however, there is much to learn, and I still come across things that make me wonder.

When I began my apprenticeship in furniture making, my boss used to talk about 'prime timber', which meant timber from just above the roots to just below the first branches of a reasonably straight tree. The grain is straight and there are no knots, so the wood is easy to work. It does not twist or warp unduly, but it is not necessarily the best in terms of appearance. In fact, it can be quite bland. Wood from other parts of the tree, which has knots, irregular colour, wild grain, and all those other so-called imperfections that are so exciting to expose, is what I am looking for.

Because wood has so many characteristics, it is described in contradictory terms. Some people say that it is an ideal material, friendly and easy to work; but others say that it is difficult to work. It has been called clean, but also described as dusty. Some people think that it is heavy, others light. The longer you work with wood, the more these contradictions become apparent.

The first word I would use to describe wood is 'unique'. Every piece is unique, so everything I turn is unique. Sometimes customers ask me to reproduce examples of my work, but while I can physically copy the shape of a bowl, it will not be the same because the piece of wood from which the original bowl is made cannot be copied.

Wood is also frustrating, because it moves, and because it has grain that can lift when it is being worked. By the time I had finished my apprenticeship as a cabinetmaker, I was well aware of how frustrating wood can be. You can produce something that fits together perfectly, is smooth and flat. Then the temperature or humidity changes and all the timber moves. Something you have spent hours working to a perfect fit no longer goes together. However, when you have learned enough about it and how to work it to overcome the frustrations, it is extremely satisfying.

The same applies to woodturning. You can make something perfectly round, but a few days later it has changed shape and there is a crack in the bottom. You can overcome such problems in any bowls you turn in the future if you can learn from what has happened. Again, that is where the satisfaction comes from.

A fascinating material

The study of timber technology, which gave a whole new perspective to my life and work, essentially concerns the structure of wood – right down to its microscopic features. I was taught the working properties of timbers, their strengths, and how to identify them. I learned about the fungi and insects that attack timber. The more I discovered about this fascinating material, the more important it became to me.

I had known all sorts of things about wood for years, but I could not have explained them before I went on the timber technology course: for example, the fact that some wood tears whichever way you plane it. It may not make much difference to know why this happens, but I find reasons comforting. It makes sense of the frustrations and heightens the satisfaction of working this material.

Understanding is really helpful when you can see just from looking at a log that one piece of wood is going to have something more exciting inside it than another, or it will have various properties that will be useful, or that can usefully be avoided.

Fig 3.1
The differences between hardwood and softwood timber.

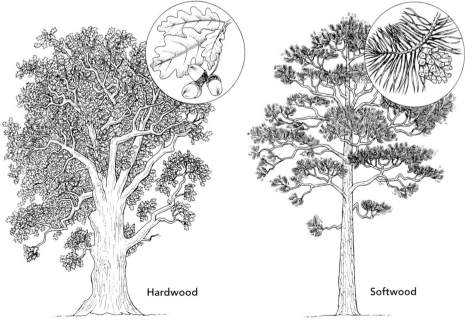

Hardwood

Softwood

For anyone who works wood, it is important to understand the differences between hardwood and softwood. First, be clear that hardwood and softwood are not the same as *hard* wood and *soft* wood. Balsawood is the classic example. It is a particularly soft wood, yet the timber trade etymologists would call it a hardwood. To understand this you have to delve into the subject.

Softwoods come from coniferous trees with needle-like leaves, whereas hardwoods come from broad-leaved trees (*see* Fig 3.1). The difference between them is that softwoods have two basic kinds of cell and hardwoods have three. Softwoods have tracheids and parenchyma cells, whereas hardwoods have vessels, fibres and parenchyma cells. In softwoods, the tracheids are arranged vertically, carrying food up and down the tree, and form the basis of the wood's structure. The parenchyma cells take food horizontally across the tree to be stored in the heartwood.

Hardwoods have two types of vertical cell: vessels, which conduct moisture up and down the tree, and fibres, which give the wood its strength and play only a minor role in distributing food. In hardwoods, the parenchyma cells also carry food horizontally into the tree where it is stored before use.

The vessels in hardwoods, and the tracheids in softwoods, can vary enormously in size depending on the time of year that they grow. They can be (relatively) big in the spring, when most growth occurs, and quite small in the summer. You can see the difference in these growth patterns in the annual rings of a tree when it has been felled.

Hardwoods tend to be easier to distinguish than softwoods because of the extra main category of cells. Sometimes, the only way to tell the wood of one conifer from another is to look at the wood under a microscope. That is why they tend to be lumped together as 'deal' by timber merchants, although there is no such tree as deal.

Fig 3.2
Reaction wood.

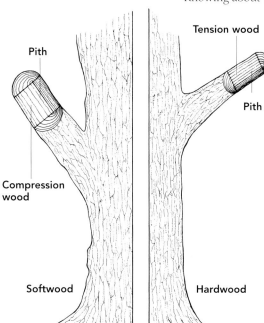

Pith

Compression wood

Softwood

Tension wood

Pith

Hardwood

Out of balance

Knowing about reaction wood is also very important in turning. Reaction wood comes in two forms: tension and compression (*see* Fig 3.2). Compression wood occurs in softwood, and tension wood is formed in hardwood. Both types of reaction wood occur naturally in the trunk of a tree when it is out of balance, such as when it grows on a hillside. They also occur in every branch. This means that there is a concentration of either cellulose or lignum, the two basic substances that comprise wood (there are other components, but these two are the most important in this case).

When the cells in wood are formed they consist of cellulose. Unlike small plants, however, which rely on the pressure of the sap to keep them upright, trees have another material – lignum – which gradually forms in the cell walls and strengthens them. Between them, cellulose and lignum give wood its particular strengths. Cellulose gives it flexibility and strength in tension, while lignum makes it hard and provides strength in compression.

A tree compensates for the imbalances of its growth by producing a particular kind of wood. In softwoods, extra growth occurs on the side that is under compression due to the imbalance (the underside of a branch, for example) and, therefore, is known as compression wood. In hardwoods the extra growth occurs where the wood is being stretched (along the top of a branch) and is known as tension wood. You can tell when reaction wood has occurred because the pith (medulla) – the middle of the growth rings – is off centre and the log takes on an oval appearance.

The extra wood formed in softwoods needs strength in compression, so the reaction wood here is high in lignum. It looks darker than the rest of the wood and is more dense. In hardwoods the opposite is the case, the wood formed being high in cellulose, which means that the fibres will lift quite easily and the wood will be more difficult to turn. When fibres lift, the wood takes on a 'woolly' texture. In both kinds of reaction wood an excessive amount of shrinkage will occur as the wood dries out. This causes a lot of movement and can lead to cracking.

Another kind of wood that moves erratically as it dries is a burr. This type of growth is caused by the tree pushing out many tiny branches that never develop properly, and can occur because of physical damage to the tree. Most trees can produce burrs, but some tend to do so more than others. Elm, walnut, oak, mulberry, and many eucalypts including jarrah, are all particularly susceptible to burring (*see* Figs 3.3 and 3.4).

Burrs are difficult to turn, and they move as they dry, often producing a textured surface. This, of course, is one of the reasons why they are turned. Another is because the grain looks exciting and attractive. By turning a burr when green, you can reduce the amount of cracking that is likely to occur as it dries. Instead it will distort, provided it is turned thinly enough.

Interesting grain patterns – called wild grain – can also be found where the tree first divides into branches (the crotch) and where branches come out of the trunk. Wild grain can also be found at the butt of the tree where the roots come together to form the trunk. Being at ground level, this area can also exhibit staining that will produce interesting effects in the wood.

Seasonal development

A tree grows by producing a series of concentric layers that develop in some seasonal way. The size and texture of these layers will vary according to the climate in which the tree grew.

On the outside of a tree is the bark, or phloem, which comprises two distinct layers. The inner layer carries food, photo-synthesized by the leaves, back down through the tree to nourish every part of it. The outer, older, layer insulates the tree against cold and heat.

Two other layers, collectively called the xylem, complete the structure of the tree. Xylem is a conducting tissue that carries nutrients up from the roots to the leaves. The outer layer is known as sapwood – the new growth. Throughout the life of a tree, new sapwood is formed. In temperate climates this occurs more rapidly in the spring than in the autumn, which accounts for the distinct growth rings. In the fairly constant weather of tropical climates, the growth rings are generally less obvious.

Fig 3.3
Large burr on a small elm tree on the roadside in Brighton.

Fig 3.4
A section of burr elm, cut ready to turn a natural-edge vase.

Between the sapwood and the inner bark is what is known as the cambium layer. This fits like a sheath over the entire tree, the cells continually dividing during the growing season and forming new sapwood and inner bark. As new sapwood is formed, the older sapwood is converted into the second part of the xylem, the heartwood, when it stops conducting moisture up the tree. As new inner bark is formed, the old inner bark becomes outer bark.

Fig 3.5
Section of an oak tree.

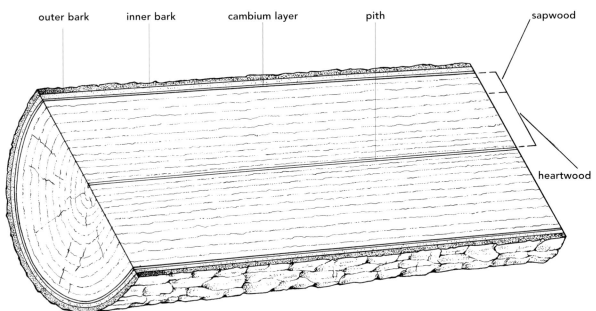

outer bark   inner bark   cambium layer   pith   sapwood

heartwood

Fig 3.6
Holm oak vase, turned dry (1983). Large medullary rays are clear to see in the side of the vase. 4in (102mm) diameter, 5in (127mm) high.

Heartwood gives a tree its strength, allowing it to stretch up towards the light needed to photosynthesize its food. When sapwood converts into heartwood, it often takes on pigments and chemicals that cause it to change colour. It was because of the difference between the light sapwood and the dark heartwood of laburnum that I started turning waney- or natural-edged laburnum bowls. I had to keep the natural edge to retain as much sapwood as possible and emphasize the difference between the heart and sap.

The parenchyma cells running across the grain of the wood take food from the bark into the cambium layer to allow the growth, and into the heartwood where it is stored. They are generally referred to as medullary rays (*see* Fig 3.6). In some woods, softwood in particular, they are only a few cells wide and hardly visible to the naked eye. In others, such as oak and London plane, they comprise large numbers of cells and form striking figuring when the wood is cut in a certain way, known as quarter sawing.

Air and water

The density of timber depends basically on the amount of air and water in relationship to the amount of wood substance. The harder and heavier a particular timber, the higher the wood substance it has. The size of the vessels or tracheids will determine this. Very dense woods will not float in water, while others – like balsa – have cells with large cavities, which make them very buoyant.

Most of the moisture contained in wood is held in the cavities of the cells that form the vessels. These are nearly full of water when the tree is growing. The rest is in the walls of the cells. As wood dries out, the moisture contained in the cell cavities evaporates first. Without this water, the wood will weigh far less – often just a quarter of its weight when it was standing. Its moisture content will then be approximately 25 per cent. Losing this moisture does not cause it to shrink, move or split, and in this state it is often known as 'shipping dry'.

Wood begins to move as moisture leaves the cell walls. Each cell shrinks, but because there are more cells on the outside of a tree than on the inside (simply because it is bigger on the outside), the wood will split if it is not cut into smaller pieces, such as boards. It will also split if it dries too quickly, because the outside will dry before the inner cells can do so. Even if it is dried slowly, it will move as the cells shrink and take up the tension caused by that shrinkage.

Although you can buy wood that is said to be seasoned, it is often only seasoned to shipping levels, so it is worth checking with the supplier. However, even fully seasoned timber often needs some further drying before you use it. For example, after rough-turning ebony blanks, I leave them to dry slowly for a further two years or more before I consider they are ready for final turning. In the interim, they are kept in a well-aired storage space, and covered in PVA (polyvinyl acetate) to prevent the moisture from evaporating too quickly and causing the wood to crack.

I like to use ebony sometimes for my work, as it allows the form I have created to stand out strongly without any distraction caused by the grain patterns of the wood. Most people think of ebony as being black, but although pure black ebony can be obtained, much of it is quite variable in colour and some can be highly figured (*see* page 86).

In hardwood, the grain is determined by the direction in which the fibres lie, while in softwood it is determined by the direction of the tracheids. Anyone who has ever planed a piece of wood will know that it will usually plane more easily and smoothly in one direction than another, and that if you turn the wood over the direction of the grain is reversed.

Some trees produce a spiral grain, the fibres tending to grow around the tree rather than straight up and down, which is often apparent on the bark (*see* Fig 3.7). When a tree has grown like this, the planks produced from it are a lot more brittle than straight-grained wood. However, it can also be a lot harder than straight-grained wood because the fibres effectively give you end grain all round.

Some trees produce spiral grain in one direction for a while, then change the direction of the spiral, producing interlocking grain. This gives the effect of dark and light strips, which can be very decorative, especially in sapele.

When the grain is interlocked, you find that whichever way you plane the wood you are lifting the grain in places. This will occur because instead of the fibres in the wood all lying in the same direction, a proportion lie in one direction and the remainder in another. This gives the wood the appearance of having light and dark areas, which change from being light (or dark) to dark (or light) when you turn the wood around. The effect is caused by the light hitting the ends of fibres, which are at different angles.

Fig 3.7
Spiral grain can be seen on this beech tree.

75

Another type of grain effect is wavy grain where the fibres themselves develop a ripple shape (*see* Fig 3.8). Cutting through these fibres produces a very decorative pattern. Although wavy grain is often easy to work, achieving a fine finish can be difficult.

While decorative grains can present problems to cabinetmakers, they are less trouble to turners who invariably have to cut against the grain at some point in their work.

Fig 3.8
The undulation of the wavy grain on this decaying log is clearly visible.

Fig 3.9
This collection of 11 boxes demonstrates the variety of colour and grain to be found in wood. Left to right: Australian grass root, ziricote, olivewood, tulipwood, cocobolo, ziricote, Honduras rosewood, cocobolo, tulipwood, African blackwood, burr elm; all 2–3in (50–75mm) in diameter.

The grain is just one of the elements that give each piece of wood its individuality. Its texture is another. The texture of wood is basically dependent on the size of the elements from which the timber is made, mostly the vessels. Large vessels will give wood an open texture, like oak, ash, ekki and iroko. These are all dense woods, but they still have an open texture. Beech, on the other hand, has a very even texture because it has small vessels. Some people call it 'close grained', but this has nothing to do with the grain, it is just because there are no big holes in the surface. Of course, individual examples from the same species can vary depending on where they were grown and how fast they grew.

Not having vessels, softwoods tend to be more even in texture. However, some display distinct differences between spring and summer growth, indicated by light and dark areas respectively. The lighter areas can be softer and more porous than the darker growth. The latter, on the other hand, often contains more resin. This difference can give the wood an uneven texture.

I do not turn much softwood, although I do use it occasionally. I turn yew, which is a softwood because of its cell structure and lack of vessels, but it certainly is not a *soft* wood. I turned a lot of Douglas fir when I was using a wire brush to make the grain stand out (*see* Fig 4.15). The wood lends itself to this treatment because there is such a difference in density between the spring and summer growth. The former is much softer than the latter, so wire brushing gives a pronounced textured finish.

Across the spectrum

The most obvious difference between pieces of wood is the colour, and there is a vast range available. It spans from the almost white of holly and sycamore to the almost black of ebony. In between, the colours range from yellow, through red, to brown. Padauk, mahogany and, from Australia, jarrah have a reddish colour. Boxwood is yellow. Walnut and laburnum have a greenish tinge, although sometimes I think the colours are in the eye of the beholder – it depends if you are looking at the wood on its own or comparing it with something else. Oak is generally considered to have a straw colour, but sometimes it has a reddish tinge.

Fig 3.10
Quarter of a ziricote log with the natural edge. The sapwood shows in sharp contrast to the dark-figured heartwood.

There is often a vast difference between the colours of the sapwood and the heartwood, the sapwood being lighter (*see* Fig 3.10). With light-coloured woods, such as sycamore, holly and beech, the difference between the sapwood and the heartwood is less distinct. In fact, it can be difficult to tell the difference. With many woods, it appears as if there is a distinct line between the darker-coloured heartwood and the lighter sapwood, but when you look more closely you will find that the line straddles an annual ring, so not all the sapwood is darkening into the heartwood at quite the same rate.

Why wood should change colour as it turns from sapwood to heartwood is a mystery. Laburnum, for example, takes up a greenish tinge, while mulberry turns a golden yellow. In England, the colour change is less pronounced than in some other countries, the wood tending to be a whitish or brownish colour, epitomized by oak. But attractive colours do appear, like the greenish tinge that can occur at the centre of ash trees and which is referred to as olive ash. Walnut sometimes has black streaks in it, while ash can pick up the same sort of colouring, which is extremely decorative.

Light-coloured woods like holly and sycamore can discolour badly during drying, especially if they are dried slowly, but the problem can be avoided by standing the wood on end to dry. Colour changes like these are the result of fungal attacks, and commonly occur when the wood is drying. The sapwood often becomes greyish, which is due to a fungus living on the food in the sapwood. In softwood, the fungus turns the sapwood slightly blue. Since deal is most frequently used in the joinery trade, it is sprayed to prevent the fungus from attacking the wood and causing the colour change, which would show through a light-coloured paint.

Fig 3.11
Above **The end of a slightly decaying beech log with spalted marking visible.**

Fig 3.12
Below **Spalted beech board, showing the patterning produced by decay.**

Fig 3.13
Bottom **I produced the spalted timber myself for this trio of vases (1985). Ash, 4in (102mm) diameter, 4in (102mm) high.**

Some fungi attack trees while they are growing; oak and chestnut are particularly susceptible to this kind of attack. One particular fungus turns oak green; others turn oak and sweet chestnut brown, either completely or in streaks interspersed with the natural wood colour. However, the incidence of these is rare (especially the green oak), so if you come across any of them you have made a valuable find.

Wood attacked by fungus that leaves black streaks and decorative discolouration in it is known as spalted timber. Beech tends to be the most commonly affected because it is susceptible to attack by fungus both when it is growing and after it has been felled (*see* Fig 3.11). It may be attacked by more than one kind of fungus, giving a variety of effects.

The most decorative effects are produced by the fungi that eventually do the most damage, breaking down the cell structure of the wood and producing zone lines as the attack moves deeper into the wood. These are the black lines you see in spalted timber. The roots, or hyphi, of the fungus sometimes only grow into the cells and fill them, causing discolouration. In most cases, fungal attack will make the wood weaker, but the degree of weakness depends on how decayed it becomes; in the right conditions it will break down completely. Allowing wood to rot in this way can be a very wasteful process, but it does produce some highly decorative effects.

Turning spalted wood can be harmful to your health, since the fungal spores may be inhaled. In the lungs they find ideal conditions for development, which can cause respiratory disease. When I turn spalted timber I always wear a face mask and use the dust-extractor system.

Fungus can only grow in moist conditions, and normally requires a moisture content of at least 20 per cent to be able to develop. To create your own spalted timber, it is best to use wood that is unseasoned. Put the wood in a plastic bag and keep it in a fairly warm atmosphere; the higher the temperature, the greater the speed of attack. A greenhouse will often produce a suitable atmosphere without the need for the plastic bag. In due course you will get spalted timber (*see* Fig 3.13). But keep an eye on its progress, as some fungi can grow

Fig 3.14
This spalted sycamore vase was made from a single log, prior to turning the laburnum vase on page 35, which is often considered my signature piece. 5½in (140 mm) diameter, 5½in (140mm) high.

Fig 3.15
Spalted birch vase (1983). Natural edge, turned dry from a triangular section cut from an irregular log. 4in (102mm) diameter, 5in (127mm) high.

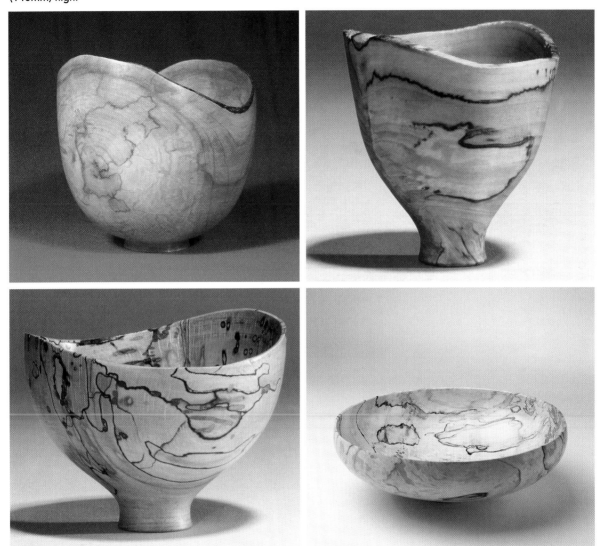

quickly and the wood can rot so much that it becomes too soft to turn. Wood spalted in this way is attractive, but spalting that has been produced by the fungus occurring naturally in the living tree always seems to produce much more vividly coloured results.

Most woods can be made spalted, but some are more susceptible to attack than others: birch, beech, horse chestnut, sycamore and walnut all decay quite readily (see Figs 3.14, 3.15, 3.16 and 3.17). Interestingly, the process will make light woods darker and dark woods lighter.

There is nothing completely new in woodturning – each generation of turners rediscovers the techniques of the past, including me. For example, I can remember when I first used spalted timber. I bought a sycamore log and

Fig 3.16
Above left Spalted beech vase (1984). Natural edge, turned dry. Woodworm attack adds to the interest of this piece. 5½in (140mm) diameter, 5½in (140mm) high.

Fig 3.17
Above right Spalted burr horse chestnut vase, turned dry (1991). The vivid zone lines caused by the fungi which attacked the wood whilst it was still growing, make this bland wood highly decorative. 10in (254mm) diameter, 3in (76mm) high.

79

Fig 3.18
Above **While I was convalescing after my heart attack, a sycamore log I had bought some time before began to decay. When I began turning again I was reluctant to waste this wood, so I used it to make this bowl, and was delighted with its appearance. I had discovered the virtues of spalted timber. Spalted sycamore, 7in (178mm) diameter, 7in (178mm) high (1982).**

Fig 3.19
Right **Vase made from a badly stained piece of yew (1986). Staining was caused by a metal object enclosed during the tree's growth. 4½in (114mm) diameter, 5½in (140mm) high.**

used some of it while it was wet and nice and white, but while I was in hospital it lay around, and by the time I was well enough to turn it the wood had started to decay. Being rather cost-conscious and not wanting to get another tree, I used the timber with the decay in it (*see* Fig 3.18). Of course, it looked wonderful, and I thought I had discovered something new. I was very pleased with myself.

Then I was given some beech that had started to decay. The first time I went to Chelsea Crafts Fair I quickly sold all the pieces I had made from it.

People found it startling. Later, I put on an exhibition at Peterborough, and the curator of the museum there asked me to look at some turned 19th century wine glass coasters to identify the wood. Clearly, they had been turned from spalted sycamore, so I had not 'discovered' spalted timber as a turning material at all. Subsequently, I discovered that some turners in the USA had also begun using it.

Making changes

There are other reasons why wood has so many colours. In addition to the refraction of light caused by changes in the grain, the annual growth rings produce their own changes in colour. Moreover, areas of unusual activity, such as burrs, produce a whole range of colours in close proximity to each other.

Unseasoned oak can change colour dramatically when in contact with iron, producing localized patches of dark purple. This also occurs in yew (*see* Fig 3.19). Sometimes you can find logs containing bits of barbed wire, nails or staples where the tree has grown over them. These areas can produce some striking colours.

You can also change the colour of the wood yourself. You can make wood look old by applying ordinary washing soda dissolved in water. That is just one of several processes used to create new colours in wood. Chemicals may be applied and allowed to react with the wood to change its colour, or it may be simply painted or stained. Woods containing quite a lot of tannin, such as oak, sweet chestnut and mahogany, can be fumed in ammonia. This simply involves putting the wood in a chamber or tent to keep the fumes contained, with a dish of concentrated (0.880) ammonia. The fumes from the ammonia will react with the tannin in the wood, causing it to darken to a warm brown. When treating wood in this way, on no account inhale the ammonia fumes, as they can be extremely painful.

Bichromate of potash is another chemical used to change the colour of wood. Again, it reacts with the tannin to produce a darker colour. Some quite startling effects can be produced by using sulphate of iron and copper sulphate. These chemicals are supplied as powders for mixing with water. Being water based, they lift the grain when they are applied, which means that the piece should be lightly rubbed down with glasspaper after they have been used.

You can also bleach wood to lighten it. Oxalic acid and ordinary domestic bleach will lighten it slightly, but if you want to bleach it nearly white you can use a proprietary two-part bleach. You can bleach walnut until it is almost as light as sycamore, and I used this treatment on a series of walnut bowls because the wood was quite bland and uninteresting. I chose a two-part bleach, which lightened the wood and gave it a slight greenish tinge.

Wood with large vessels, i.e. 'open-grained' wood, can be limed by rubbing lime wax over it after it has been lightly coloured (*see* Fig 3.20). In recent times, this has become a fashionable finish for kitchen cabinets.

The use of stains on turned work has become quite popular. I did go through a period when I stained some of my work, but at the time the range of stains available was limited and the colours tended to be too bright for my taste. Spirit, oil and water-based stains are available, although the last will lift the grain and require further sanding when dried. Spirit stains soak in deeply

Fig 3.20
Limed oak coopered bowl (1978). After turning the outside, it was planed flat to produce sloping facets. The turned base was added afterwards. 12in (305mm) diameter, 4½in (114mm) high.

and dry very quickly. Oil stains, however, take longer to dry which can be an advantage, allowing a more even colour to be achieved. They soak in quite deeply, but may react with some lacquers applied subsequently.

As time goes by, the natural colours in wood gradually lose much of their sparkle, becoming more mellow. Exposure to sunlight will hasten the change, some woods darkening slightly and others becoming bleached. Despite this, there is so much natural beauty in wood that I no longer believe it can be enhanced by changing or hiding its colour. Nowadays all I want to do is give the wood a form that shows its beauty to the best advantage.

A wide choice

I use a variety of woods for the bowls, vases and boxes I make, each having its own colour, grain variation and other individual properties. They include well-known native British timbers, such as oak, sweet chestnut, ash, sycamore, elm, walnut, lime, acacia and yew, as well as the less common woods such as laburnum, mulberry, sumach and judaswood. Then there are the fruit woods, such as apple, pear, cherry, plum and damson. I also use a wide variety of rare and exotic woods from around the world, some of which are highly decorative.

English oak is straw coloured with large medullary rays that add greatly to the interest of the wood. Turned green, it becomes quite textured due to these rays and the varying density of the annual rings. When the dark bark is incorporated in the design, it makes a striking contrast to the lighter wood. Oak is easily turned but, due to its open texture, is difficult to finish to a high gloss. **Burr oak** is also quite widely available, the wild grain adding to the interest of this wood, especially for bowls and vases.

Holm oak is an evergreen oak. When freshly cut, it is a whitish stone colour, but as it ages it mellows and the colour becomes warmer, similar to ordinary oak. It has a high proportion of horizontal tissues, which produce very large, distinct rays, especially on the end grain. Because of these, the wood becomes very textured when turned green.

Sweet chestnut is similar to oak in colour, but does not have the large medullary rays. It is easily turned and lends itself to being fumed. When exposed to strong ammonia fumes, it changes to a nice warm brown.

Sycamore is a very light-coloured wood; if dried correctly, it has an even, creamy white colour. **Holly** is the only British wood that is whiter than sycamore. It is also slightly harder. Both are easily turned and ideal for turning green. This permits bowl walls to be made very thin while ensuring that the wood dries quickly, allowing you to keep them as white as possible.

I seldom use **straight-grain elm**, but **burr elm** is one of my favourites. It has a warm brown colour with many variations due to the growth of the knots. It is suitable for both green and dry turning. The former often produces interesting shapes, the wood distorting as it dries (*see* Fig 3.21). When turned dry, burr elm can be given an excellent finish.

English walnut is greenish brown, often with darker-coloured streaks that may be nearly black. The sapwood is a light creamy colour. This wood turns well, and a superb surface finish can be achieved. Because the wood absorbs a great deal of heat, extra care should be taken when sanding the finished turned pieces, otherwise surface cracking is likely to appear. English walnut is much more decorative than its American counterpart, **American black walnut**.

Fig 3.21
Above Burr elm vase (1990).
Natural edge, turned green. A
piece of included bark
provided interest in the form
of a fault. As the wood dried,
the fault opened up to
produce a striking feature.
11in (279mm) diameter, 6in
(152mm) high.

Fig 3.22
Far left Spalted burr horse
chestnut vase, turned dry
(1992). 4in (102mm) diameter,
3in (76mm) high.

Fig 3.23
Left Robinia vase, turned dry
after rough turning (1990).
The open texture makes this
an easily recognizable wood.
10½in (267mm) diameter, 5½in
(140mm) high.

Woods such as **beech**, **horse chestnut** and **ash** are normally quite bland in colour. I often use them in their spalted state, however. Beech, with its striking black lines, is the most common, although for me, horse chestnut produces the best spalted wood (*see* Fig 3.22). It displays a wide range of colours: blacks, browns, reds, greys and creams. Ash is not readily available in spalted form, but when it is it can be very decorative indeed.

Lime is a fairly soft wood, but is very stable. Unfortunately, it has a somewhat bland appearance, and it is generally used for carving. Sometimes burred pieces can be found, which is when this wood becomes more interesting to the turner. If turned thin, the burring allows the light to shine through, showing up some exciting grain patterns.

Robinia, often called acacia, should more correctly be called false acacia. An open-grained wood, it is much darker in colour than oak. It is easily turned and finishes well (*see* Fig 3.23).

Over the years, I have used a number of rarer woods grown in Britain, one of these being **laburnum**. This could be considered my signature wood, as I have often exploited the sharp contrast between its sapwood and heartwood. When laburnum is green, the sapwood is a creamy colour, but it can turn quite grey as it dries. The heartwood is a greenish brown, darkening to quite a deep brown. The bark can provide an extra contrast, the inner bark being creamy in colour, whereas the outer bark is greenish brown. Laburnum can be turned both green and dry. When dry, it can be very hard indeed, but an excellent finish can be achieved. Two main species of laburnum are available: one has a far deeper and decorative grain pattern than the other.

Mulberry is not readily available, but this golden-coloured wood is very easy to turn. It is a wood that exhibits many defects, while small burrs often grow on the branches and parts of the trunk. The defects and burrs give the wood much added excitement.

Fig 3.24
Above **Cocobolo vase, turned dry after rough turning (1994). 4in (102mm) diameter, 4in (102mm) high.**

Fig 3.25
Right **African blackwood vase with a natural edge (1992). 5in (127mm) diameter, 5½in (140mm) high.**

Sumach is a small tree grown for ornamental purposes, but it produces a highly figured wood, probably the most decorative wood grown in Britain. Bright greenish brown in colour, with darker and lighter streaks, it has a whitish sapwood. It is best turned green, as this wood is quite soft and becomes woolly when dried, making it difficult to finish. Other ornamental trees also produce wood that is suitable for turning. Two of these, which are extremely decorative, are **judaswood** and **Portuguese laurel**.

The fruit woods all turn well and are even textured. However, they have quite a high shrinkage rate, and if left in log form will soon develop radial splits. **Cherry** is a light yellowish brown, sometimes with a pinkish or reddish tinge. **Pear** is blander and has a light pinkish brown colour. It is very easily turned and finished. **Apple** is whitish in colour with a pinkish tinge. **Plum** and the closely-related **damson** produce wood that can vary in colour from light yellowish brown to a deep reddish brown. The colour seems to be associated with the fruit: the darker they are, the darker the wood. Damson is the darkest and displays interesting variations in the grain pattern. The sapwood of both plum and damson is a creamy colour.

The more exotic woods I use come from overseas. Most **ebony** is now imported from Africa, although occasionally pieces may come from India and Sri Lanka. **Macassar ebony**, however, comes from Indonesia. Mexico and other South American countries provide **rosewoods** and **ziricote**, while Australia supplies **jarrah** in burr form and other **eucalyptus burrs**, **mountain ash**, **grey gum**, **York gum** and **Australian grassroot**. **Olivewood** and **briar roots** come from Spain, and Africa provides **African blackwood** and **bubinga**.

Many of these are very hard woods with a fairly even texture, but their hardness makes them quite difficult to turn. Often they are extremely abrasive to tools, and as a result much time can be spent sharpening your turning tools. However, an excellent finish can be obtained with all of them.

There are several **rosewoods** to choose from, some being true rosewoods (*Dalbergias*), others being given the name because they look similar. At one time **Brazilian rosewood** was the most common, but it has been over-exploited and, rightly, is no longer exported.

There are four true rosewoods that are sold under other names. They are all very decorative, and are worth seeking out: **cocobolo** is the most decorative of the rosewoods, every piece seeming to have a character all of its own. The colour may vary from deep red to yellow with irregular veins of purple or black (*see* Fig 3.24). **Kingwood** and **tulipwood** are also highly decorative. Kingwood is violet-brown with dark streaks, while tulipwood has a heartwood in irregularly-striped colours, varying from yellow, through rose, to violet. **African blackwood** is a hard and heavy blackwood with a purple tinge. Used widely in the manufacture of musical instruments, it has a creamy sapwood that has great decorative possibilities (*see* Fig 3.25).

The other true rosewoods are not so attractive. **Honduras**, for example, can be very variable. Some pieces may be a warm reddish brown and quite bland, whereas others can have dark stripes, making the wood very decorative. **Indian rosewood**, a dark purple blackwood, has a far more open texture than the other rosewoods. It is also now available from plantations in Indonesia, being sold under the name **sonokeling**. The colour of this is often more variable, ranging from dark purple-brown to light brown with blue and green tinges.

A number of other woods have also been given the name rosewood, although they are not true rosewoods. No doubt, this is a commercial ploy to boost their sales. **Santos rosewood** is quite a decorative wood. Its colour ranges from a pinkish brown to a darker violet-brown with streaks of varying colours. **Bubinga** is also known as **African rosewood**. A hard and even-textured wood, it often has interlocking grain. The wood is light reddish brown in colour with darker coloured figuring. Although it is hard to turn, an excellent finish can be obtained. **Mexican rosewood** is the other name for **bocote**, which is a golden brown in colour with darker streaks. As it matures, the colour darkens to a warmer brown, and the figuring becomes less distinct. Although hard, it turns and finishes very well.

Bocote is closely related to **ziricote**, which is an extremely decorative wood with a very exciting grain pattern (*see* Fig 3.26).

Fig 3.26
Natural-edge ziricote vase, turned dry (1990). The creamy sapwood produces a striking contrast with the dark heartwood. 9in (229mm) diameter, 4½in (114mm) high.

Fig 3.27
Above left **African ebony vase, turned dry after rough turning (1994). 6in (152mm) diameter, 3½in (89mm) high.**

Fig 3.28
Above right **Burr jarrah vase, turned green (1989). The surface became very textured as the vase dried. 6½in (165mm) diameter, 7in (178mm) high.**

It is dark greyish brown in colour with dark lines. Although these are associated with the growth rings, they do not always follow them closely and can change direction abruptly. This wood is very dusty and dirty to work. It is also rather brittle, and there is a great risk of surface splitting as it dries. However, a fine surface finish can be achieved.

Many people have the false impression that **ebony** is pure in colour without any figuring at all. This is probably due to the fact that, since the 18th century, much of the ebony used has been stained and further lacquered black, a process known as ebonizing. The reason was to produce wood of a consistent colour.

Sri Lankan ebony is probably the blackest and also the hardest. Often this wood shows narrow, lighter greyish or brownish strips. **African ebony** is not so consistent in colour. Although some pieces can be jet black, others have lighter strips and flashes (*see* Fig 3.27). **Macassar ebony** is a very decorative wood, being black with lighter figuring. Like all the other ebonies, it is very hard and can be given a very fine finish. All are very dusty and dirty to work; the dust from macassar can cause serious nasal problems.

In recent years, a wide variety of decorative woods has been imported into Britain from Australia, many of them especially for woodturning. Probably the most popular is **jarrah** in burr form, which is highly decorative. The colour varies from a dark pink to a deep red, the many knots being darker. When dry, this wood can be very hard indeed, and quite difficult to turn. When green, however, it is quite easy to turn. As it dries, the surface develops an exciting texture (*see* Fig 3.28).

Many other forms of burr **eucalyptus** are also imported, and most are extremely decorative woods. **Grey gum** is a deep red colour with a pinkish sapwood (*see* Fig 3.29), while **York gum** is a warm brown colour with a dark cream sapwood. This gives a very tasteful contrast. **Flood gum** is another reddish burr, and **salmon gum** is a reddish brown. The list goes on, with various **gimlet gum** burrs, **myrtle** and **musk** burrs. All are turned because of their decorative properties.

Mountain ash is another eucalyptus burr. It has a high shrinkage rate, so it distorts greatly as it dries. For many years, plain mountain ash has been imported into Britain under the name Tasmanian oak. This wood is similar in colour to English oak, and is often used for parquet flooring.

The **grassroot** tree is commonly known in Australia as blackboy. This plant is classified as one of the lily family, and when growing, it looks like a small palm tree. The grasses grow in a clump from the top of the stem, which projects above the ground (*see* Fig 3.30). This wood is rather soft. For added interest, it can be turned to incorporate the textured top edge (*see* Fig 3.31). The growth rings are easily distinguished, the wood varying in colour from a light to warm brown. In time, it will darken slightly. Grassroot is easy to turn, but the dust from it can be a serious irritant, so great care should be taken when using it. It is always best turned while wet, as this helps reduce the dust problem slightly.

Fig 3.29
Top A slice of grey gum burr, showing the sapwood and bark.

Fig 3.30
Above **Australian grassroot: the broad area in the foreground is the top of the trunk from which the grasses grow.**

Fig 3.31
Left **Australian grassroot vase, turned green, with a natural edge and a slightly textured surface (1992). 8in (203mm) diameter, 4½in (114mm) high.**

Fig 3.32
Above left **Briar vase with a natural edge, turned green (1990). Stones can often be found in briar root, and when removed they leave holes which can make interesting features. 10in (254mm) diameter, 5½in (140mm) high.**

Fig 3.33
Above right **Olivewood vase with bark edge, turned semi-dry (1993). This vase contains three hearts within it because it was turned from a forked log. The two projecting pieces are part of small branches which grew on the log. 11in (279mm) diameter, 7in (178mm) high.**

Spanish olivewood comes from a small, gnarled tree. The wood is very variable in colour, generally being a light yellowish brown with darker figuring that produces a very decorative wood (*see* Fig 3.33). Because of its gnarled growth, many of the logs are irregularly shaped with very interesting figuring within them. Olivewood is easy to turn, but although it is an even-textured wood, achieving a fine finish can be difficult due to the large amount of resin within the wood.

Briar, which produces a large bulbous root system just under the ground, is a very interesting wood to turn. It is best turned when freshly dug up, but can cause difficulties due to the stones and sand that can become in-grown as the root enlarges (*see* Fig 3.32). Briar is light pink in colour, but this darkens to a much warmer brown on exposure to the light.

Although there are hundreds of woods from Africa, I find many of them bland and unexciting to turn. The mahoganies hold no excitement for me at all. However, in addition to African blackwood, ebony and bubinga, I also use **wenge** and **padauk**.

Wenge has a very prominent growth ring pattern, the very dense part of the ring contrasting with the softer and lighter part. When green, the wood can be quite creamy in colour, but as it dries and the surface is exposed to the light, it becomes a dark warm brown.

Padauk is another wood with a strong colour, being bright orange when first cut. However, this darkens to a reddish brown on exposure. It is a fairly hard wood with an open texture, and is ideal for producing thin-walled vessels when turned dry (*see* Fig 3.34).

The woods mentioned here are but a few of those I use regularly – when they are available. Of course, there are many thousands to choose from, and as time goes by, I become aware of yet more woods to turn. Although I have described some woods as bland, it pays to keep an open mind, as sometimes I find logs that are exceptions to the rule, proving exciting and interesting to turn.

Fig 3.34
African padauk vase, turned
dry and rough turned (1994).
This shows a striking contrast
between the reddish brown
heartwood and the creamy-
coloured sapwood, which has
been slightly attacked by
fungus. This is evident from
the bluish patches and the
dark zone lines. 8in (203mm)
diameter, 4¾in (121mm) high.

④Techniques

As with any occupation, woodturning involves acquiring a range of basic skills, but those skills are merely a starting point. They must be perfected and used as a basis for experimentation if your work is truly to express your own personality.

When it comes to woodturning, the term 'technique' has two distinct aspects: one is the dexterity, or skill, involved in the manipulation of tools and equipment; the other is choosing a particular process in favour of another. There are no hard and fast rules for developing woodturning techniques; often, it is just a question of finding a way of doing something that suits you. For example, the techniques I use are particularly suited to turning the thin-walled, smoothly finished pieces I like to make.

I am a great believer in letting the lathe do the work. Turning requires far less effort, and I have far more control, when the lathe is running at maximum speed. By that I do not mean revolving as fast as it can, but rather spinning as fast as the piece will allow before it starts vibrating. With a big lump of dense, irregular wood, that will be quite slow. As the wood is worked, the irregularities in it are removed and it becomes more balanced, allowing the speed of the lathe to be increased. When a bowl is nearly finished, it could be turning at the maximum speed of the lathe.

Most of my bowls and vases are turned using a pair of high-speed steel bowl gouges, one ground straight across and the other ground with a fingernail point on it. I have several of these in sizes ranging from ¼–⅝in (6–16mm), and I tend to use the smaller ones most, especially for the insides of vessels. I prefer to have fine shavings coming off quickly due to the speed of the lathe than large shavings coming off slowly. With a high speed and a small gouge, I do not have to push hard on the work, which not only enables me to turn vessels with thin walls, but also means that they can be secured to the lathe with much lighter chucking methods.

Having said that, however, when I am working on the outside of a bowl or vase, which is held by a screw chuck, faceplate or any other method that holds the blank firmly and securely, I often find it better to use a large gouge with a wide bevel so that I can produce a nice even curve. When you use thinner gouges on the inside, there can be a problem with the tool vibrating. To overcome this, you have to keep the rest very close to the work, but this is not always possible, so it may be necessary to use a thicker gouge.

Getting started

When the wood has been mounted on the lathe, the first process is to rough it out, starting with the outside of the vessel (*see* Fig 4.3). I usually do this with one of the larger gouges that are ground straight across, using the centre of the gouge. As the wood takes on a regular and even shape, I speed up the lathe so that the shavings will come off more quickly and with less effort.

Once the outside has been turned to the shape I want, I produce a cleaner cut, using the straight side of the gouge pushed quite hard against the work. This gives a smoother and more regular cut. I often finish off with a scraper to remove any little ridges and raised grain before starting to sand.

Fig 4.1
Top **A dry, forked log of olivewood.**

Fig 4.2
Above **The olivewood fork is bandsawn to a rough shape before being turned. Because the fork is used, a vase with three hearts in it will be produced. The diameter of the visible end of the log is approximately 6in (152mm).**

Fig 4.3
Left **The olivewood blank mounted on the lathe, being rough turned.**

Fig 4.4
Left bottom **Continuing the turning using a ⅝in (16mm) bowl gouge ground straight across.**

I sand the work with various grades of abrasive paper or cloth, often starting with as coarse a grade as 60 grit aluminium oxide, and finishing with something as fine as 1000 grit silicon carbide. Usually, I complete the outside, including polishing, before turning the piece round to take out the inside (*see* Fig 4.7).

It is generally thought that to make a thin-walled bowl, you start by making one with thick walls, then gradually reduce them until you reach the required thickness. However, this technique will only be successful if the bowl is comparatively small in diameter and fairly shallow, with walls no less than ⅛in (3mm) thick. Furthermore, the wood should be completely dry.

The correct approach is to make a thin-walled bowl from the beginning, working in steps from the top to the bottom. First the rim is turned to the required thickness, then more waste is removed and another portion of the walls turned to the correct thickness. You continue removing the waste in steps until the bowl is completed. It is also advisable to sand in steps in the same way.

The reason for working in this manner is that the thin wall needs material below to support it while it is being turned. If not, the bowl will flex, causing the tool to dig in, and more likely than not, the bowl will shatter.

When you remove the inside of a bowl, you also release stresses from within the wood, which have a tendency to make it move, causing the bowl to become slightly oval. Therefore, if you leave the sanding process until you have finished the walls, the result is likely to be a rim that is uneven in thickness. Sanding in steps helps to minimize this problem. The larger the diameter of bowl, the more it is likely to flex. Of course, the degree of flexing will vary, depending on the type of wood, its state and moisture content. However, even seasoned wood can pull itself inwards when the inside is removed and the tension in the outer layers no longer has anything to support it. I always sand the top section before I move on, to make sure that the rim has an even thickness.

If I am making a flat-topped bowl (as opposed to one with a natural edge), I start by making sure the top is flat, using the straight-ground gouge with the bevel rubbing and cutting just off the centre of the gouge. I often find it an advantage to use the gouge as a drill to make a hole in the blank down to a certain depth. The reason is that the centre of the bowl is the most difficult to remove because the wood at that point is moving quite slowly. If you become too aggressive in attempting to remove it, you can easily knock the bowl off the chuck. Before you begin drilling, you have to make a small depression, otherwise the blank will be thrown off the lathe. The gouge is eased to the horizontal position and pushed. Often, it needs withdrawing to clear the waste material before it can be pushed to the required depth.

Once I have decided on the thickness of the bowl's walls – which

Fig 4.5
Top A ¼in (6mm) bowl gouge ground to a fingernail shape has been used to turn the small foot. Now a ¼in (6mm) bowl gouge ground straight across is carefully used to finalize the outside shape.

Fig 4.6
Bottom A dome scraper is used to finish the foot of the vase.

92

depends a lot on the wood, although it would be unusual for mine to be more than ⅛in (3mm) thick – I use the straight-ground gouge to remove the waste from the centre, working back towards the wall of the vessel. Then I use the fingernail-ground gouge to reduce the wall to the required thickness down to a depth of ¾in (19mm) or so. More wood is removed from the centre with the straight-ground gouge, and the next section of the wall is reduced to the required thickness with the fingernail gouge. I continue in this way until I reach the bottom of the bowl, where I may use the straight-ground gouge to finish off, depending on the shape of the piece.

When I began turning, my fingertips were sensitive enough to determine the thickness of a bowl's walls, but after so much turning they have become tougher and less sensitive. So these days I use callipers to make sure that the walls are of uniform thickness. Callipers are also more accurate for measuring the thickness of a vessel's walls where they curve – an area that can deceive your fingertips by seeming thicker than it actually is. My aim is to achieve the same thickness all the way down. There is a great risk of making the walls thinner towards the bottom of the bowl, as the wood nearest the chuck has more support and, therefore, is easier to cut with less effort. Without care, you can actually cut the bottom right out of the bowl.

Your own choice

Turning, like any other method of cutting wood, requires sharp tools, but many people worry too much about such details as the angle of the bevel and the sweep of the gouge. In my experience, these are not critical. The correct angle of the bevel is whatever suits you, just so long as you keep it rubbing on the wood while you are working. Do not be afraid to adjust your tools to your own way of working and to the pieces you are making.

In deciding on the bevel angle, remember that the more acute the angle, the sharper the edge and the finer the cut. On the other hand, an acute-angled bevel will lose its edge quicker than a more obtusely ground bevel. When turning hard, exotic woods, do not use too acute a cutting angle, as you will spend more time sharpening your gouges than you do cutting with them. On the other hand, turners do become used to their gouges having a particular angle on them and reach a compromise. I do not measure the angle I grind my gouges to, but the bevels are about 45°. After a while, achieving the bevel angle you want becomes second nature.

One of the golden rules of turning is that you keep the bevel of your gouge rubbing on the wood when you are cutting with it. However, when you become competent, you realize that there are times when the bevel of the gouge cannot rub against the workpiece – for example, when the shape of the bowl

Fig 4.7
Top **After turning the outside, the vase is sanded and lacquered and allowed to dry prior to being reversed.**

Fig 4.8
Middle **With the foot held in a spigot chuck, the vase is centred to make sure it turns true.**

Fig 4.9
Bottom **The inside is turned out using a ¼in (6mm) bowl gouge ground straight across.**

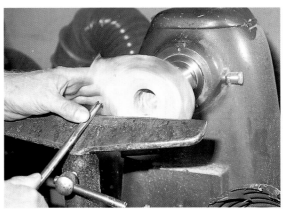

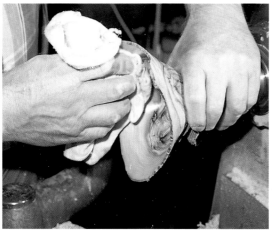

Fig 4.10
Top **The inside is gradually removed.**

Fig 4.11
Middle **The inside wall of the vase is gently scraped to remove the small ridges.**

Fig 4.12
Bottom **After sanding, the vase is lacquered and polished.**

is such that you need to turn a sharp corner when you reach the bottom. Using a gouge in this way is not advisable, as there is the risk of a dig-in, which could ruin the work or even dislodge it from the chuck, but it may be the only way to achieve the desired result.

The accepted method of treating a scraper is that it should be ground at about 80° and then have a burr put on it, as if it was a cabinet scraper. This makes it impossible to use the scraper with the bevel rubbing; you have to use it with the handle above the horizontal and the cut being made by a small burr on the back of the blade. However, I do not believe that the burr does much cutting; as soon as it is pushed against a piece of hard wood spinning at 2000 rpm, that burr is worn away and what is actually doing the cutting is the back of the blade. If the blade is doing the cutting anyway, why not make the blade sharper? You can do that by giving the tool a more acute angle on the bevel.

Consequently, my scrapers have much the same bevel angle as my gouges (around 45°), and far from putting a burr on them, I stone off the top edge after I have ground them to remove any burr there might be, which I do not do after grinding my other tools. This makes my scrapers probably the sharpest tools I use.

I actually use a scraper in two ways: in the traditional manner, that is, horizontally at the bottom of boxes and vases; but more often in the same way as you would a skew chisel, with the handle down, the bevel rubbing and the blade presented to the wood at an angle. Using scrapers in this way is becoming more popular these days, the technique now being called sheer scraping, although in reality it is cutting rather than scraping.

When you are using a scraper in the more traditional horizontal position, there are two golden rules: when scraping the outside of a bowl, the rest should be positioned so that the scraper edge is below the centre-line of the bowl; when scraping inside, the rest should be positioned so that the tool is above the centre-line. This prevents dig-ins because there is virtually no wood under the tool in each case.

When I am turning the inside of a bowl, I hold the gouge in my right hand and support the work with my left hand, behind the point where the tool is cutting. I do not press on the wood to such an extent that I burn my fingers, but just provide some support. There are two reasons for doing this: one is that it strengthens the area being cut and helps prevent vibration; the other is that it helps support the wood on the chuck because many of my pieces overhang the chuck considerably.

Drying time

I often rough turn a bowl so that the walls are ¾–1½in (19–38mm) thick, then leave the wood to dry before completing the work. The thickness depends on the size of the bowl, the wood and its shrinkage rate. Sometimes I will leave these blanks for up to three years before I finish the bowl. Woods like ebony and some of the other exotics take a long time to dry. Sycamore, on the other hand, can be ready in just six months without any force drying.

When drying wood, I often paint the end grain with PVA glue to prevent it from drying out more quickly than the rest of the wood and splitting; I coat the outside of blanks completely (*see* Fig 4.14). It reduces the risk of cracking in end grain.

It is difficult to determine exactly when a piece of wood is ready to be turned; I rely on experience and a certain amount of intuition. Sometimes things go wrong and I turn a piece that I know is not really ready because there are pressures on me to turn something for a gallery or an exhibition. Usually, I am proved right and the wood moves.

Sometimes, however, it may be desirable for the wood to move, so I turn it green. Green wood is readily available, and it is a lot easier to turn than seasoned wood because it is softer.

Most failures or problems occur when you try to turn wood that is in a semi-seasoned state. If wood is really green, i.e. freshly sawn down, it has a lot of moisture to lose from inside the cells before the cell walls start drying

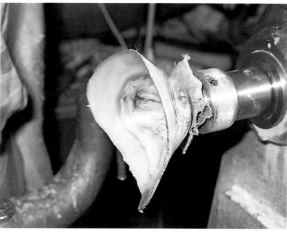

Fig 4.13
The finished vase prior to its removal from the lathe.

Fig 4.14
A section of burr elm, rough turned, coated with PVA glue and left to dry.

out and the wood moves. If it is properly seasoned, the cell walls have dried out and there should not be any more movement due to loss of moisture (although there may be some due to the release of tensions). In between is that state where most of the water has evaporated from inside the cells, but the walls are still wet. If you turn it in that state, the heat caused by friction between the wood and the tools will quickly dry out the cell walls. A lot of movement will occur, and the wood will shrink and twist; it is also likely to develop heat shakes, which are small cracks caused by the surface of the wood drying out too quickly.

Whether you are turning smooth-edged or natural-edged bowls, the techniques are the same. When turning natural-edged bowls or wood with holes in it, using the lathe at high speed and the tools with little pressure on them will ensure that there is less likelihood of pushing the tool in and catching the edge on any irregularity. It also gives you much better control.

The right lathe

When choosing a lathe, the most important consideration is that it should have good bearings so that the work does not vibrate. For the same reason, the lathe must be firm, either because it is heavy or because it is fixed down securely. Moreover, the bigger the pieces you are going to turn, the heavier your lathe needs to be, especially if you are going to turn irregularly shaped pieces.

One important development, as far as my work is concerned, is the advent of bowl-turning lathes using the inboard side. That means the workpiece is turning towards you, in the same way as it does when you are spindle turning between centres. Turning on the outboard side of a lathe means you have to cut the wood on the right hand side of the bowl. If you are right handed and holding your gouges in the most natural and comfortable way, you cannot support the work with your left hand when you are turning like this. Although you do tend to become ambidextrous with experience, holding the tool with my left hand and supporting the work with my right is not the easiest way of working for me.

The generally accepted rules of woodturning tend to originate from spindle turners, because when turning began to be popular as a hobby in the mid-1970s, most of the books on the subject had been written by spindle turners, who did not have the lathes, tools or chucks that are available today. One of the main criteria of my work is to achieve a smooth finish with no tool marks on it, and to do that I make considerable use of abrasive papers, beginning with particularly coarse papers, such as 80 or even 60 grit, and progressing to finer papers. However, that contradicts the generally accepted spindle turning practice of applying the turning tool heavily so that the bevel will burnish the wood behind the cut and leave little, if any, finishing necessary with abrasives. The reason for my approach is that you cannot push hard on a vessel that has a wall thickness of ⅛in (3mm) or less, especially when it is made from some of the more decorative or wild-grained timbers.

In spindle turning, the wood is normally mounted with the grain running the length of the lathe, but when I am turning a bowl, the grain runs across the axis of the lathe. Because of this, there are two points where I am cutting directly against it, which has a tendency to lift the grain. This occurs on both inner and outer surfaces of the bowl.

Careful tool work is required to keep grain lifting to a minimum; sometimes the gentle use of a scraper can help to ease the problem, but excessive use will make it substantially worse. After the scraper, coarse sanding should remove, and smooth, the areas of raised grain. I start with a coarse (60–80) grit because it generates a lot less heat than a fine grit. After the coarse grit, I work through the grades – 100, 120, 150, 180, 220, 320, 500, 1000 – to achieve the finish I want. Using this method reduces the risk of heat shakes, because the abrasives are not in contact with the wood long enough for them to become too hot.

Abrasives work by cutting, and blunt abrasives generate heat because they rub without doing much cutting. The excessive use of abrasives can cause dust to build up on the sheet, which will also cause heat. In addition to melting animal glues on the abrasive sheet, this build-up of heat can cause resins and oils from the wood to polish the surface, making it difficult to apply a finish.

Power sanding can speed up the process, allowing lifted grain to be smoothed quickly, much quicker than when sanding by hand. It is ideal for the outside of bowls and vases, and the inside of large bowls. An abrasive disc is mounted in an electric drill and applied to the workpiece while it is spinning on the lathe. The discs come in a variety of sizes and grits; I use the 2in (51mm) size in grits down to 400, then finish off by hand.

However, you have to be careful when power sanding. With woods that have uneven textures or soft spots, such as spalted timber, it is easy to produce a very uneven surface to the workpiece. Care must also be taken when sanding natural-edged bowls or vases, as holding the disc at the wrong angle will result in an uneven edge.

A textured finish

Although nowadays I like my work to be smooth to bring out the beauty of the grain, in the past I have used various methods to produce textured finishes. Certain woods, especially the softwoods (Douglas fir is ideal), have quite a distinct variation in their annual rings (*see* Fig 4.15). The spring growth is lighter in colour than the summer growth. Because it is also softer, it can be worn away more easily than the summer growth, giving the wood an undulating finish. You see this effect in driftwood that has been in the sea for some time, and you can achieve it for yourself by using a wire brush. This can be applied while the wood is turning if the grain is at right angles to the lathe, or when you have stopped the lathe if you are turning into end grain.

Another way of achieving an undulating finish with the summer growth standing proud of the spring growth is to burn the surface of the wood with a blow torch. This will darken the wood and leave carbon deposits that will need cleaning off afterwards, which can be done with a wire brush, either

Fig 4.15
Douglas fir coopered bowl (1978). The outside was brushed to make the summer wood stand proud. 10in (254mm) diameter, 3½in (89mm) high.

hand-held or as an attachment to a drill or flexible drive (*see* Fig 4.16). Different areas will need different amounts of flame; end grain will be harder to burn than long grain. As you become more experienced, you will discover how much of the wood to burn for the best effect. Of course, this will vary greatly, depending on the type of wood used.

Regardless of the surface, you will probably want to seal the wood and give it a certain amount of polish with an applied finish. It is important to remember that this will not hide any tool or sanding marks left on the wood, or make a rough surface smooth. In fact, it will tend to highlight any imperfections. A really good finish has to be achieved before the surface coating is applied.

Fig 4.16
For a while I experimented with burning and wire brushing my work to give a textured finish; the smooth finish inside provided a pleasing contrast. Elm, 10in (254mm), diameter, 3½in (89mm) high (1977).

As with abrasives, there are many finishes to choose from. Among those available are oils that can be applied in several coats, each being allowed to dry before applying the next. The main disadvantage of oils is that they are slow drying and will only provide a matt surface finish. Many will leach out of the wood, leaving the surface a little sticky and attracting dust. Danish oil is one oil that will not leach out, once it has dried, and it provides a fairly hard surface finish. Several coats can be applied to build up a silky sheen, but this can be a lengthy process, as the oil may take quite a long time to dry, depending on the wood.

Olive and other vegetable oils can be also used, and many a salad bowl has been finished in olive oil because there is no danger of the finish contaminating the food. The bowl can be cleaned easily by wiping and maintained by the occasional wipe over with more olive oil. However, certain vegetable oils can become rancid in time.

Wax can also be used, and can be applied over other finishes. Various types are often mixed together to provide a workable consistency. For example, beeswax and carnauba (a vegetable wax) are often melted together in white spirit or turpentine. The proportions of the waxes can be as much as 50–50, although about 10 per cent of carnauba is usually considered enough. About the same volume of white spirit is added as the melted waxes mix together. For safety, the wax and spirit are best melted together in a two-part boiler, such as a tin can in a saucepan of water.

The mixture can be left to dry to a block, and then applied directly to the revolving workpiece. As the heat of friction melts the wax, it fills the grain and can be burnished later to a mirror-like finish. Another method is to thin the wax further with more spirit and use it as a paste, burnishing the workpiece with a cloth.

Beeswax is far too heavy for me; I prefer a thinner wax with less body in it. I use one of the modern silicone wax polishes, of which there are many brands available.

Another popular finish is sanding sealer, which is available both as a shellac-based product (shellac is dissolved in methylated spirit) and as a cellulose material, which usually needs to be thinned with a cellulose thinner. Sanding sealers also include a sanding lubricant to reduce clogging of abrasives and prolong their lives.

Shellac takes much longer to dry than the cellulose sealer – several hours as opposed to half an hour, depending on the conditions – and it can also discolour the wood slightly. On the other hand, it is more compatible with other finishes that may be applied after the sanding sealer, which was developed as a base for other finishes, such as polyurethane and melamine lacquers. Cellulose will lift some oil-based stains, giving a streaky finish. Water stains, however, tend to be compatible with most other finishes, but they are slow to dry and they do lift the grain.

I generally apply a thin coat of cellulose sanding sealer, which is allowed to dry for 15 minutes or more. Then I sand it down to remove the small ribs than can occur on the surface, after which the piece is waxed and burnished to give a slight sheen. On a wire-brushed or burnt surface, it would make sense to apply a spray finish and perhaps polish with wax, taking care to remove any excess wax from the troughs, otherwise it will show.

I do not like the high-gloss appearance that you get with a build-up of several coats of a polyurethane or melamine finish. These plastic finishes are resistant to heat and water, but as I am turning decorative pieces that are unlikely to be subjected to either, fortunately I do not need to use them.

Methods of chucking

There are many different ways of holding the workpiece on the lathe, and which you choose depends on what you are trying to achieve. The *safest* way to turn a bowl is with a big chuck that is secured to as much surface area as possible, and to turn it as slowly as possible. However, this will not necessarily produce the best bowl.

Long before I took woodturning seriously, I heard about a man who used brass screws to secure a piece of wood to the faceplate of his lathe. With the lathe running, the screws sheared, and the workpiece flew off, causing him serious injury. For a while that worried me, and I filled every hole in my faceplate with steel screws, even drilling extra holes for more screws. It did not take me too long to get over this fear, however, and realize that even quite hefty pieces of wood could be held perfectly safely with relatively light fixings, as long as I did not put too much pressure on those fixings, and the piece was balanced properly. That realization led me on to increasing lathe speeds, lighter use of tools and progressively thinner walls to my bowls. Even so, it is not a bad thing to be concerned about securing the workpiece to the chuck;

it is far better to be safe than sorry, and most accidents occur when people become overconfident.

In most cases I use only a single screw in a screw chuck to hold the wood, but I do at times employ a variety of chucking methods, because using only one is too restrictive. In days gone by, turners would produce bowls with just one chucking. The screws of the faceplate were driven into what would become the base of the bowl, and the outside and inside of the work would be turned with the wood held in that way. Almost inevitably, this resulted in a heavy and clumsy-looking bowl.

Knowing the different methods of chucking, and having a selection of chucks at your disposal, gives you so much more freedom of expression when it comes to deciding on the shape of a bowl. What is not acceptable is tailoring your work to your chuck. You should not be dictated to in that way. When you want to achieve something, you have to find a way of doing it.

My methods of chucking include faceplates, screw chucks, the modern collet and spigot chucks, home-made jam chucks, and three- and four-jaw chucks. Rarely do I use anything bigger than a 6in (152mm) faceplate, and I turn bowls up to 20in (508mm) in diameter on that. Otherwise, I use 3 or 4in (76 or 102mm) faceplates. When I use a screw chuck, I rely on the single screw in the centre for fixing. Screw chucks do have two other holes in them for further screws, but I tend not to use them unless I am turning something larger than usual, or I am being particularly ambitious by turning something like a very soft spalted piece of timber.

Fig 4.17
English walnut, part dried, rough turned and coated with PVA glue. It will be left for about a year to dry completely. The centre has been grooved out to relieve the stresses as it dries.

Recent years have seen the development of parallel screws in screw chucks. Although many turners swear by them, I have never found them to be as good as people say they are, so I tend to employ the old-fashioned screw chuck, which I find much easier to use. You can change the length of the screw from a short one for hard, exotic timbers to a long one for soft burrs or spalted timber. If the wood does not feel firm enough, or you are turning a large piece of timber, you can add the extra two screws. I would not turn an 18in (457mm) bowl on a single screw, but anything up to 14in (356mm) can be held with the centre screw only, provided the blank is of regular shape and consideration is given to the speed at which the blank revolves.

A pin chuck is another means of holding a blank when turning the outside of a bowl or vase. It is ideal for turning a natural-edged bowl where it is not easy to attach a faceplate or screw chuck to the uneven surface of what will be the natural edge. Of course, the blank must be thick enough to take the depth of the pin, and the hole must be drilled accurately to match as closely as possible the size of the chuck.

The pin chuck itself comprises a metal dowel with a flat on it. The dowel is pushed into a hole drilled in the blank, and the pin – also of metal – is inserted in the gap left by the flat. As the blank revolves, the pin is forced to one side, holding the wood firmly in position. Unfortunately, with the single pin, it is difficult to stop the wood from vibrating slightly. Also, if too much pressure is applied when cutting, especially if the wood is soft, the pin chuck will revolve in the blank, preventing it from being driven. Although this is a quick and cheap method of chucking, it is not easy to get right.

Another method is to use an expanding straight-sided spigot chuck. This has a central dowel like a pin chuck, but once this has been inserted into the pre-drilled hole, jaws are opened up. There is a good ⅛in (3mm) of movement, and the chuck holds the wood much more firmly than is possible with a normal pin chuck, so I tend to favour it over the latter.

While I am turning the outside of a vessel, I have to take into account the method of chucking I will use when the bowl is turned round to finish the inside. This does not influence the shapes I make because I find ways of chucking the forms I want to produce, but this does have to be worked out in advance.

Sometimes I will put a recess into the base so that I can use an expansion chuck for holding the work while I turn the inside (*see* Figs 4.17 to 4.22). Quite often I will glue another piece of wood to the outside of the bowl before I start to turn it so that this can be held in a spigot chuck while I turn the inside. Then I reverse it onto a jam chuck to finish off the bottom.

The extra wood, usually plywood, is fixed to the bottom with a thick cyanoacrylate adhesive, commonly known as superglue (*see* Figs 4.23 to 4.25). This can be used with an accelerator, which will also clean off any grease or oil on the wood. Alternatively, water is a good accelerator, making superglue cure even more quickly than normal.

Fig 4.18
Top **The outside has been remounted and turned; the foot is being marked for a recess.**

Fig 4.19
Middle **The shape of the foot is gradually formed.**

Fig 4.20
Bottom **A recess in the base being turned out. Although this recess will be a part of the foot, it is also used to hold the bowl with an expanding chuck when it is reversed.**

Fig 4.21
Continuing to turn the outside
of the bowl.

Fig 4.22
The bowl reversed and the
top edge being turned using a
¼in (6mm) bowl gouge with a
fingernail point. Turning down
in stages.

Turning the extra piece of wood off afterwards means reverse chucking the bowl. This can be done in several ways, but I do it by fixing a piece of wood or man-made board to a faceplate and turning a recess, the perimeter of which is a tight fit on the outer rim of the bowl. The latter can then be jammed onto this chuck and the bottom finished off.

Another method is to make the recess fit the inner rim of the bowl, which works with thick-walled bowls, but there is a danger that it will split a thin-walled vessel. Either way, the tools need to be controlled carefully to avoid knocking the work off the chuck. One way of reducing this risk is to bring the tailstock up to hold the workpiece in place, but I do not usually find this necessary.

On many of my vases and bowls, I form a small foot while turning the outside, and hold this foot in a spigot chuck when I come to turn the inside. This foot is either finished off as part of the piece, or turned off later. I have a range of spigot chucks from ½in (13mm) up to 3in (76mm), and I can always make chucks of intermediate sizes if necessary.

Although I do not do much spindle turning, I tend to think of the boxes and goblets I make as spindle work because the grain of the wood runs in the same direction as the bed of the lathe. Also, some of this turning is performed between centres at the headstock and tailstock ends of the lathe.

For turning boxes and goblets, different kinds of chucks and centres are used because the work has to be supported without the tailstock, as well as with it. A three- or four-jaw chuck will hold the workpiece at the headstock end even when the tailstock is removed, which is necessary for hollowing out a goblet or box. I often finish the outside after hollowing out, especially with goblets, because they have a thin stem, and the wood would not support the cup section while it was hollowed out if I made the stem first.

Fig 4.23
Above An ebony blank which was rough turned two years before and left to dry. The outside is now being re-turned.

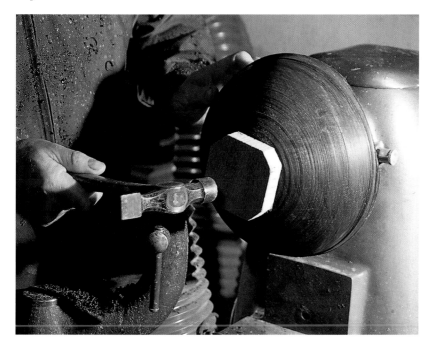

Fig 4.24
A block of laminboard has been glued to the base using a thick cyanoacrylate adhesive.

Fig 4.25
The block being turned so that the bowl can be reversed and held in a large spigot chuck (see page 140 for completed bowl).

Fig 4.26
This goblet shows the annual
rings of the original Australian
grassroot. 4in (102mm)
diameter, 6½in (165mm) high.

With the cup hollowed out, I turn a plug for the tailstock, which can be pushed into the cup to hold the workpiece while the outside of the goblet is formed.

Three-jaw, self-centring engineering chucks have been used in this method of turning for many years, as have the four-jaw versions, which tend to have single adjustable jaws. The extra jaw in the four-jaw chuck gives more gripping surface, and the recent introduction of a self-centring type at an economic price has led to an increase in their popularity. With either type, it is wise to keep the overhang of the jaws to a minimum, as catching your fingers on them while they revolve is painful.

Natural-edge and green turning

A natural-edged vessel is one that uses the natural outside edge of the tree, branch or log, or the outside of a burr, to produce an uneven top rim. The bark may still be attached if the wood is in the correct condition when it is turned. Many people associate turning natural-edged bowls with green turning. This association is natural enough because green wood is ideal to exploit in this way, and many natural-edged pieces are made from it.

The reason for using green wood is because a lot of timbers develop radial shakes, or cracks, on the edges as they dry out. This is less likely to occur if the wood is turned while it is green because a lot of the stresses are removed as wood is taken out during turning. You have to turn the wood fairly thin or it could still crack as it dries; the maximum is about ¼in (6mm). Green wood is also easier to cut, and any tendency for the grain to lift will be reduced.

The wood will still shrink as it dries out, and it will move, which is why vessels that are turned from wet wood are often irregular by the time they have dried. However, as the turned wood shrinks it can distort the shape without splitting, as long as the walls are thin enough.

You can predict how an object that has been turned while it is wet will move as it dries out. For example, it will tend to become oval because it shrinks more across the grain than it does along the grain. If you want to emphasize that change, you turn the wood to encourage it to move in that way, considering the positions in which the annual rings lie and bearing in mind that annual rings become shorter as they dry. A knot will stand proud once wet-turned wood has dried, so you can incorporate a textured finish to the piece by using that knowledge. A burr is a whole tangle of knots that are partially formed small branches, which will create a highly textured, as well as decorative, finish once it has been turned and has dried out. This textured finish is not only visually exciting, but also makes the piece more tactile.

I often keep the bark on a bowl because it adds a contrasting texture to a smoothly finished vessel as well as additional colour variations. To do this, the wood must be turned while it is wet, practically straight from the tree. Once the cambium layer begins to turn grey, which can be quite quickly, the bark will start to separate from the wood and eventually fall off. Some people stick the bark back on with superglue, but that seems to me to be losing the essence of the material you are using.

If you turn the wood before the cambium layer has started to deteriorate, there will be no deterioration afterwards. The heat caused by friction between the tools and the spinning wood begins to dry the wood, and thin-walled vessels will dry out quickly anyway. Once the wood is dry, the fungus that causes the deterioration cannot attack the cambium layer.

If the wood is in the correct condition when turned, the joint between the wood and the bark will be as strong as the bark itself. The bark is always weaker than the wood, but if the wood is turned when it has been freshly cut, the bark is an integral part of the log. Some woods, such as beech and oak, have a strong mechanical bond with the bark because there are large rays running through to the bark. Even when the cambium layer is diseased, the bark of these woods may remain in place for a considerable time, although eventually it will come adrift.

Fig 4.27
Its three hearts and creamy
sapwood border contrasting
with the brownish heartwood,
make this dry-turned, natural-
edge laburnum vase a highly
figured piece. 11in (279mm)
diameter, 6in (152mm) high
(1994).

Some woods that are turned while wet feel completely different when
dry to the same wood that has been dried and then turned. The wet wood
dries very quickly when turned, and surface tension is set up in the piece. The
surface becomes slightly case hardened because the cells stretch, making the
surface of the wood harder and smoother than normal.

Natural-edge turning not only offers that interesting rim, but it also
provides the contrast between the sapwood and the heartwood, which is what
originally led me to this technique. When I started using some dry laburnum
logs, I wanted to keep the sapwood, so I developed my technique for turning
in this way. There is a strong contrast between the sapwood and heartwood of
laburnum, making it an ideal material for turning with a natural edge (*see* Fig
4.27). It has a greenish brown heartwood and a creamy yellow sapwood. This
contrast provides an added dimension to turned work, giving it a border
around the top of anything from ¼–1in (6–25mm) wide.

The simplest way of turning a natural-edged bowl is to start by sawing
a log lengthways through the heart, and then cutting a length of the halved
log a little longer than the diameter of the log (*see* Fig 4.28). Mount this on
the lathe using a pin chuck, screw chuck or even a faceplate, depending on
the size of the piece of the wood, with the rounded natural edge fixed to the
chuck. It is most important to position it evenly, because the two sides of the
finished work need to be fairly similar and the piece should be evenly
balanced when you turn it round to remove the inside. Many of my pieces
have a small foot, which is often held in a chuck while the inside of the vessel

is being removed. If the wood was not mounted evenly originally, it will be unbalanced and the foot will not be able to hold it while the inside is turned. Having said that, there are times when I want one side to be longer than the other to show the grain to its best advantage, perhaps because there is some feature I want to emphasize. I have to take that into consideration when I am turning the piece, and I might have to work at lower speeds on the lathe than I would be able to if the wood was even.

One important consideration when turning a natural-edged bowl is that the shape is still paramount (*see* Figs 4.29 to 4.31). That is why I judge the shape while the wood is turning. When it is spinning, you can see the overall shape – it does not look as if it has an irregular edge. If the shape is pleasing while spinning, it will be pleasing when the work is finished and on display. The natural edge is simply an enhancement that you have to try to incorporate into the overall design. Sometimes the natural edge may not make the form of the spinning piece look quite right, so then I judge the form at a line below the natural edge, which can be made easier by applying a ring of masking tape.

Fig 4.28
Above Blank of half a 6in (152mm) laburnum log, drilled so it can be held by an expanding pin chuck.

Fig 4.29
The blank is mounted on the chuck, then turned to shape using a ⅝in (16mm) bowl gouge.

Fig 4.30
Once turned to shape, the outer surface is gently scraped using the bevel of the scraper pushed hard against the wood to remove the small ridges.

Fig 4.31
The completed outside shape turned and sanded.

That is the interesting work. Turning the inside is the same as with any other bowl. It is quite a mundane task, and simply a question of removing the wood and making sure the walls are of a uniform thickness (*see* Figs 4.32 to 4.34). The only difference between turning the inside of a natural-edged bowl and any other bowl is that the piece may not necessarily balance, so care must be taken to ensure that the bowl is square in the chuck and revolving centrally. If out of balance, it can pull out, or the sides of the bowl may be of uneven thickness, which on a very thin bowl is quite noticeable. You begin removing the inside with the lathe running slowly, but as the wood is removed, you can speed it up because there is less weight to pull the piece out of square.

Of course, when you start you must be careful on the irregular top edge, holding the tools firmly, but making light cuts. You also have to be careful when sanding a natural-edged bowl, because the top edge is rough and uneven, and at ¹⁄₁₆in (1.5mm) thick it can be as sharp as a saw. It is very easy to break a bowl when sanding the inside, as the paper can become caught by the irregular edge.

If I turn a natural-edged bowl or vase on a spigot, for obvious reasons it is not possible to fix it to a jam chuck to allow removal of the spigot once the inside is finished. Instead, I cushion the edge with a small rubber or foam pad glued to a piece of wood mounted on the chuck. Alternatively, I might use a pad and support the inside of the bowl against the tailstock. Then I bring up the tailstock to support the end. In this way, I can turn the spigot down to a very fine spindle that still touches the tailstock. That spindle is taken off when the work has been removed from the lathe.

Some of the natural-edged bowls or vases I turn have the complete heart running through them. By using a branch that has other branches coming off it, you can get the heart of each branch showing in the finished piece. I have turned vessels with three, four or even five hearts showing. When you are turning a piece of wood like that, you have to pay particular attention to mounting it on the lathe so that you end up with the hearts showing in the finished work exactly where you want them. To do that, you need to know what is inside the wood, which comes with experience.

Of course, green turning can be applied to bowls that do not have natural edges. It is much more important to consider how the annual rings are situated in the piece, so that you can make sure the piece distorts in a certain way. This will depend on the shape you want, and also on the grain formation.

Fig 4.32
Top **With the vase reversed and held by the small foot in a spigot chuck, the inside is carefully turned using a ¼in (6mm) bowl gouge, ground straight across.**

Fig 4.33
Middle **The turning continues: the speed that the piece is revolving is gradually increased as it becomes more balanced.**

Fig 4.34
Bottom **The fine edge is finished. Turning down to the base in stages.**

Fig. 4.35
The finished laburnum vase.
Note the three distinct
layers: bark edge, sapwood
and heartwood.

Gallery Two

I have turned twenty bowls especially for this book. These are the culmination of many years' experience, and demonstrate the current level of my work. All have been produced during the past two years (1993–1995).

A wide variety of woods has been used, some from as far afield as Australia (burr jarrah and grassroot), Mexico (cocobolo and ziricote) and Africa (blackwood and pink ivory wood). I have also made use of Spanish olivewood, as well as many English woods, including yew, sycamore, laburnum, burr elm and two diseased woods, namely spalted beech and spalted horse chestnut.

In all cases I have tried to match the design to the wood. Some of the pieces have been turned to incorporate the natural edges of the log, while others are much more formal in shape.

A vast difference in surface finish has been achieved. Some of the pieces have been turned from green wood, and as it has dried the surface has become textured; this is very evident in some of the burr wood pieces. Others have been rough turned and allowed to dry for at least a further year; these will tend to be more even in shape and have a smooth surface. The harder woods, such as ebony and cocobolo, are particularly shiny due to their fine texture.

The thickness of the walls varies slightly, depending on the type of wood and the size of the vessel. Average thickness is $\frac{1}{12}$in (2mm).

Below
Ziricote bowl. Turned dry after rough turning. A very decorative bowl produced using this highly figured, dark wood from Mexico. 10in (254mm) diameter, 3¼in (83mm) high.

Top left
The fineness of the top edge.

Left
Close up of the startling black figuring.

Opposite
Laburnum vase. Turned dry. This vase is turned from part of a log where the log has divided into two. By doing this, three hearts are included in the vase. The sapwood borders the top rim and the foot, its creamy colour is a sharp contrast with the rich brown heartwood. 5½in (140mm) diameter, 5½in (140mm) high.

Left
Showing the contour of the edge and the way the sapwood borders it.

Below
The detailed figuring at the junction of the two hearts.

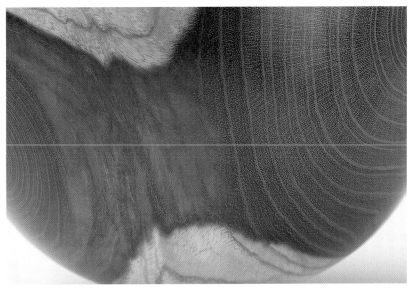

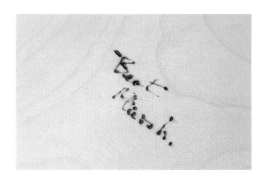

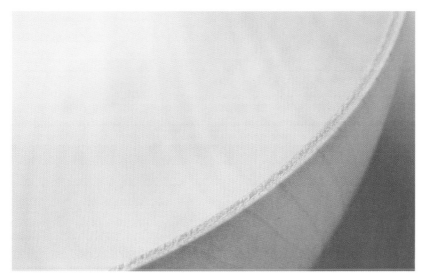

Opposite
Sycamore bowl. Turned dry after rough turning. This bowl has been turned with no foot, and due to the lack of pigment in the wood, the bowl is translucent. 10½in (266mm) diameter, 5in (127mm) high.

Top
Underside of the bowl with no foot, with my signature across it.

Bottom
Detail of the top edge which has a cove in it.

Opposite
Burr elm vase. Natural edge,
turned green. The creamy
sapwood around the top edge
gives a striking contrast to the
warm brown of the rest of the
vase. 7in (178mm) diameter,
5¾in (146mm) high.

Below
Close up of the fine natural
edge.

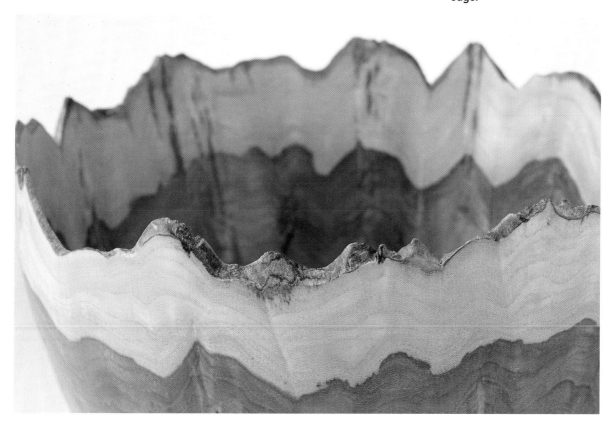

Opposite
Yew bowl. Turned dry after
rough turning. The inclusion of
the sapwood in this bowl
provides two further points of
interest. 9½in (229mm)
diameter, 4½in (114mm) high.

Above
Close up of one patch of
sapwood and the fine top
edge of the bowl.

Left
The other area of sapwood on
the opposite side of the bowl.

Opposite
Cocobolo vase. Turned dry after rough turning. The addition of a small piece of sapwood near the foot adds to the interest of this vase. 8in (203mm) diameter, 4¼in (108mm) high.

Left
Close up of the foot and the patch of sapwood.

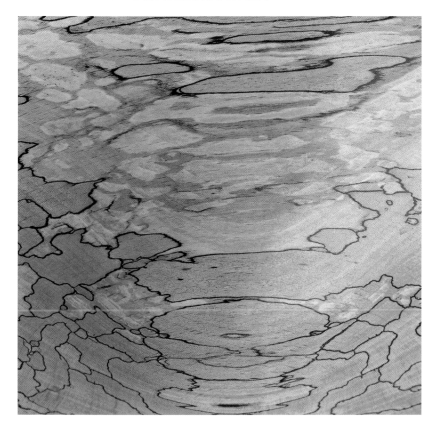

Opposite
Spalted beech bowl. Turned
dry after rough turning. The
dark zone line markings make
the bowl highly decorative.
12½in (317mm) diameter, 3½in
(89mm) high.

Top
The bowl in full profile.

Bottom
Close up of the spalted
figuring of this wood.

Opposite
Burr elm vase. Natural edge, turned green. After drying, the numerous small knots all over this piece give an exciting texture. 13in (330mm) diameter, 7½in (190mm) high.

Left
Close up of the top edge showing its fineness and irregularity.

Opposite top
Ebony vase. Turned dry after rough turning. This nearly black vase shows off the shape with very few other distractions to the eye. 5½in (140mm) diameter, 3¼in (83mm) high.

Opposite bottom
The vase in full profile.

Left
Close up of the foot.

Opposite
Olivewood vase. Turned partly dry. Made from a very highly figured piece of wood. The heart of the log is running across the vase. 6½in (165mm) diameter, 6½in (165mm) high.

Top
Another view of this vase.

Bottom
Close up of the heart showing the exciting figuring.

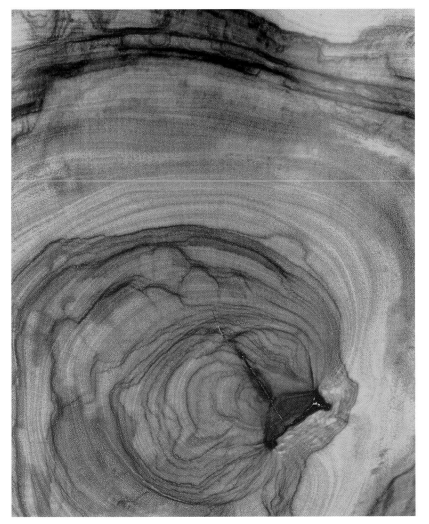

Above
Burr elm bowl. Turned semi-
dry after rough turning. Made
from an exceptional piece of
burr elm with numerous small
knots clustered all over the
wood. 15in (381mm) diameter,
5in (127mm) high.

Right
Detail of the top edge and
close up on the various knots.

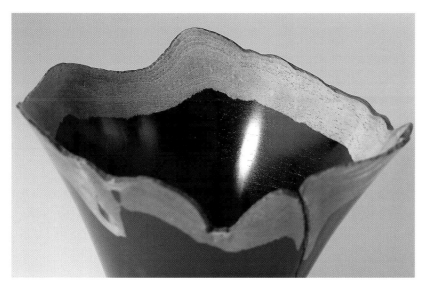

Above
African blackwood vase. Natural edge, turned dry. Although virtually black, blackwood is still a highly figured wood, set off by the contrasting creamy sapwood bordering the top edge. 5in (127mm) diameter, 4½in (114mm) high.

Left
Close up of the top edge and the bordering sapwood.

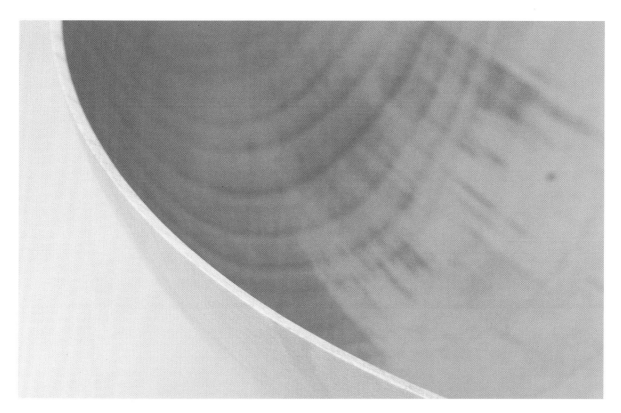

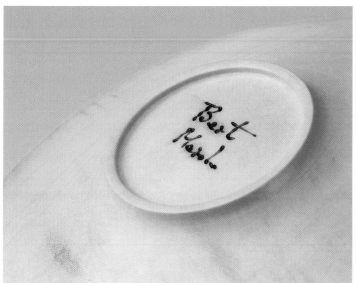

Opposite
Sycamore bowl. Turned dry
after rough turning. A nearly
white, translucent bowl with
greyish marking. 11½in
(292mm) diameter, 4½in
(114mm) high.

Above
Detail of the sharp top edge.

Left
Close up of the foot which has
been hollowed out to achieve
a much more balanced bowl.

Opposite
Cocobolo bowl. Turned dry after rough turning. This is a very decorative bowl with no foot and a completely round underside. 6in (152mm) diameter, 4in (102mm) high.

Left
The completely round underside of the bowl.

Opposite
Australian grassroot vase. Natural edge, turned green. The growth rings and storage rays are visible. When dry these rays stand proud giving the piece a decorative, textured surface. 10½in (266mm) diameter, 9¼in (235mm) high.

Top
Close up of the foot, also highlighting the textured surface.

Bottom
Detail of the fine top edge.

Opposite
Pink ivory vase. Turned dry
after rough turning. The fine
finish on this vase shows the
extraordinary colour of pink
ivory wood. 4½in (114mm)
diameter, 4¼in (108mm) high.

Left
Close up of the attractive
figuring caused by the wavy
grain.

Opposite
Ebony bowl. Turned dry after rough turning. The simplicity of the form is accentuated by the near blackness of this piece. 9in (229mm) diameter, 4in (102mm) high.

Top
Detail of the top edge and the carefully turned hollow.

Bottom
Close up of the hollowed foot.

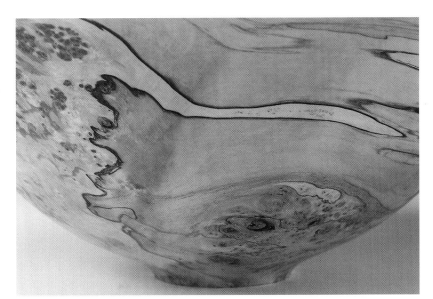

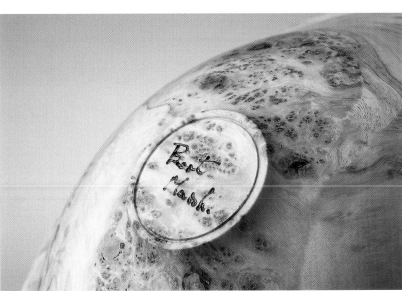

Opposite
Spalted burr horse chestnut vase. Turned dry after rough turning. The astonishing array of colours and patterns caused by the fungal attack, together with the clusters of small knots, combine to make this a very conspicuous vase. 11in (279mm) diameter, 4in (102mm) high.

Top
Striking zone lines.

Bottom
Close up of foot showing burr figuring.

Above
Burr elm vase. Turned dry after rough turning. The warm brown contrasts with the darker knots, given emphasis by the smooth surface finish. 15in (381mm) diameter, 5¼in (133mm) high.

Right
Close up of the foot.

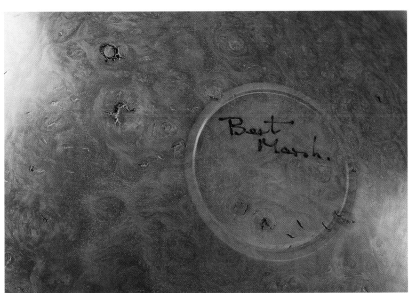

Above
Burr jarrah vase. Turned semi-dry after rough turning. The simple shape of this bowl is complemented by the highly burr-figured wood with its slight texture. 13in (330mm) diameter, 7½in (190mm) high.

Left
Detail showing the base of this piece.

Index

GMC PUBLICATIONS

BOOKS

WOODTURNING

Adventures in Woodturning	*David Springett*	Practical Tips for Turners & Carvers	*GMC Publications*
Bert Marsh: Woodturner	*Bert Marsh*	Practical Tips for Woodturners	*GMC Publications*
Bill Jones' Notes from the Turning Shop	*Bill Jones*	Spindle Turning	*GMC Publications*
Bill Jones' Further Notes from the Turning Shop	*Bill Jones*	Turning Miniatures in Wood	*John Sainsbury*
Carving on Turning	*Chris Pye*	Turning Wooden Toys	*Terry Lawrence*
Colouring Techniques for Woodturners	*Jan Sanders*	Understanding Woodturning	*Ann & Bob Phillips*
Decorative Techniques for Woodturners	*Hilary Bowen*	Useful Woodturning Projects	*GMC Publications*
Faceplate Turning: Features, Projects, Practice	*GMC Publications*	Woodturning: A Foundation Course	*Keith Rowley*
Green Woodwork	*Mike Abbott*	Woodturning Jewellery	*Hilary Bowen*
Illustrated Woodturning Techniques	*John Hunnex*	Woodturning Masterclass	*Tony Boase*
Keith Rowley's Woodturning Projects	*Keith Rowley*	Woodturning: A Source Book of Shapes	*John Hunnex*
Make Money from Woodturning	*Ann & Bob Phillips*	Woodturning Techniques	*GMC Publications*
Multi-Centre Woodturning	*Ray Hopper*	Woodturning Wizardry	*David Springett*
Pleasure & Profit from Woodturning	*Reg Sherwin*		

WOODCARVING

The Art of the Woodcarver	*GMC Publications*	Understanding Woodcarving	*GMC Publications*
Carving Birds & Beasts	*GMC Publications*	Wildfowl Carving Volume 1	*Jim Pearce*
Carving Realistic Birds	*David Tippey*	Wildfowl Carving Volume 2	*Jim Pearce*
Carving on Turning	*Chris Pye*	The Woodcarvers	*GMC Publications*
Decorative Woodcarving	*Jeremy Williams*	Woodcarving: A Complete Course	*Ron Butterfield*
Essential Woodcarving Techniques	*Dick Onians*	Woodcarving for Beginners: Projects, Techniques & Tools	
Lettercarving in Wood	*Chris Pye*		*GMC Publications*
Practical Tips for Turners & Carvers	*GMC Publications*	Woodcarving Tools, Materials & Equipment	*Chris Pye*

PLANS, PROJECTS, TOOLS & THE WORKSHOP

The Incredible Router	*Jeremy Broun*	Sharpening Pocket Reference Book	*Jim Kingshott*
Making & Modifying Woodworking Tools	*Jim Kingshott*	The Workshop	*Jim Kingshott*
Sharpening: The Complete Guide	*Jim Kingshott*		

TOYS & MINIATURES

Designing & Making Wooden Toys	*Terry Kelly*	Making Wooden Toys & Games	*Jeff & Jennie Loader*
Fun to Make Wooden Toys & Games	*Jeff & Jennie Loader*	Miniature Needlepoint Carpets	*Janet Granger*
Making Board, Peg & Dice Games	*Jeff & Jennie Loader*	Turning Miniatures in Wood	*John Sainsbury*
Making Little Boxes from Wood	*John Bennett*	Turning Wooden Toys	*Terry Lawrence*

CREATIVE CRAFTS

Celtic Knotwork Designs	*Sheila Sturrock*	Embroidery Tips & Hints	*Harold Hayes*
Collage from Seeds, Leaves and Flowers	*Joan Carver*	Making Knitwear Fit	*Pat Ashforth & Steve Plummer*
The Complete Pyrography	*Stephen Poole*	Miniature Needlepoint Carpets	*Janet Granger*
Creating Knitwear Designs	*Pat Ashforth & Steve Plummer*	Tatting Collage	*Lindsay Rogers*
Cross Stitch on Colour	*Sheena Rogers*		

UPHOLSTERY AND FURNITURE

Care & Repair	*GMC Publications*	Making Shaker Furniture	*Barry Jackson*
Complete Woodfinishing	*Ian Hosker*	Pine Furniture Projects	*Dave Mackenzie*
Furniture Projects	*Rod Wales*	Seat Weaving (Practical Crafts)	*Ricky Holdstock*
Furniture Restoration (Practical Crafts)	*Kevin Jan Bonner*	Upholsterer's Pocket Reference Book	*David James*
Furniture Restoration & Repair for Beginners	*Kevin Jan Bonner*	Upholstery: A Complete Course	*David James*
Green Woodwork	*Mike Abbott*	Upholstery: Techniques & Projects	*David James*
Making Fine Furniture	*Tom Darby*	Woodfinishing Handbook (Practical Crafts)	*Ian Hosker*

DOLLS' HOUSES & DOLLS' HOUSE FURNITURE

Architecture for Dolls' Houses	*Joyce Percival*	Making Period Dolls' House Accessories	*Andrea Barham*
A Beginners' Guide to the Dolls' House Hobby	*Jean Nisbett*	Making Period Dolls' House Furniture	*Derek & Sheila Rowbottom*
The Complete Dolls' House Book	*Jean Nisbett*	Making Victorian Dolls' House Furniture	*Patricia King*
Easy-to-Make Dolls' House Accessories	*Andrea Barham*	Miniature Needlepoint Carpets	*Janet Granger*
Make Your Own Dolls' House Furniture	*Maurice Harper*	The Secrets of the Dolls' House Makers	*Jean Nisbett*
Making Dolls' House Furniture	*Patricia King*		

OTHER BOOKS

Guide to Marketing	*GMC Publications*	Woodworkers' Career & Educational Source Book	*GMC Publications*

VIDEOS

Carving a Figure: The Female Form	*Ray Gonzalez*	Woodturning: A Foundation Course	*Keith Rowley*
The Traditional Upholstery Workshop		Elliptical Turning	*David Springett*
Part 1: *Drop-in & Pinstuffed Seats*	*David James*	Woodturning Wizardry	*David Springett*
The Traditional Upholstery Workshop		Turning Between Centres: The Basics	*Dennis White*
Part 2: *Stuffover Upholstery*	*David James*	Turning Bowls	*Dennis White*
Hollow Turning	*John Jordan*	Boxes, Goblets & Screw Threads	*Dennis White*
Bowl Turning	*John Jordan*	Novelties & Projects	*Dennis White*
Sharpening Turning & Carving Tools	*Jim Kingshott*	Classic Profiles	*Dennis White*
Sharpening the Professional Way	*Jim Kingshott*	Twists & Advanced Turning	*Dennis White*

MAGAZINES

WOODTURNING • WOODCARVING • TOYMAKING
FURNITURE & CABINETMAKING • BUSINESSMATTERS
CREATIVE IDEAS FOR THE HOME

The above represents a full list of all titles currently published or scheduled to be published. All are available direct from the Publishers or through bookshops, newsagents and specialist retailers. To place an order, or to obtain a complete catalogue, contact:

GMC Publications, 166 High Street, Lewes, East Sussex BN7 1XU United Kingdom
Tel: 01273 488005 Fax: 01273 478606

Orders by credit card are accepted